An Introduction to **Art Education**

Roger Clark

The University of Western Ontario

Plan B Books
142 Chestnut Hill
London, Ontario
Canada
N6K 4J6
(519) 641-4551

Layout and design: Roger Clark

Canadian Cataloguing in Publication Data

Clark, Roger Allen, 1953-
    An introduction to art education

Includes bibliographical references.
ISBN 0-9683450-0-X

    1. Art--Study and teaching. I. Title.

N85.C55 1998   707'.1   C98-900289-6

First Printing May, 1998

Published by Plan B Books.
Printed and bound in Canada by Aylmer Express Ltd., Aylmer, Ontario.

ACKNOWLEDGEMENTS

I would like to sincerely thank the following individuals and groups for their génerous assistance in the preparation of this book:

ART
Dennis Burton
kerry ferris
John MacGregor
Bob Zarski
Todd

COPYRIGHT
Canadian Society for Education through Art
John Henry Martin
McIntosh Gallery, The University of Western Ontario

CONTENT
John Henry Martin
Catherine Elliot Shaw

TECHNICAL
Michelle Barrett
Media Services, Faculty of Education, The University of Western Ontario

ENCOURAGEMENT
Derek & Patsy Allison
Tom & Debbie Anderson
Howard Craven
Peder & Valerie Nielsen

Every effort has been made to trace the ownership of all copyrighted material in this book and to obtain permission for its use. ∎

CONTENTS

C.1
ROGER CLARK
Genesis Revisited 1982
Plaster and vermiculite
66 x 46 cm.
Collection of the artist

PRACTICE

ART EDUCATION ORGANIZATIONS

- **Provincial**
  Art Council of the Newfoundland
      Teachers' Association
  Art Teachers' Association of Nova Scotia
  Art Teachers of Prince Edward Island
  Association Québécois des Éducateurs
      et Éducatrices Spécialises en Art
      Plastiques
  British Columbia Art Teachers'
      Association
  Fine Arts Council of the Alberta
      Teachers' Federation
  Manitoba Association for Art Education
  New Brunswick Art Education Council
  Ontario Society for Education through
      Art
  Provincial Association of Art Teachers
  Saskatchewan Society for Education
      through Art

- **Canadian**
  Canadian Society for Education through
      Art

- **United States**
  National Art Education Association
  United States Society for Education
      through Art

- **International**
  International Society for Education
      though Art

An Introduction to
ART EDUCATION

The educated lead the world.
We conclude from this that, next to parents,
teachers collectively hold more power than anyone in society.
The power of visual language was lost to the West a long time ago.
Its dormancy is one of our greatest losses,
unappreciated as such because people today do not miss what they never had.
They fail to note the difference between a frill subject and a subject of untapped power.[1]
Dennis Fehr

TEACHING AS AN ACT OF COURAGE

It takes courage to create. According to Rollo May, there are many kinds of courage: physical, moral, and social, but the most important of all is the **courage to create** which requires an encounter between the subjective self and the objective world.

Teaching is itself a creative act that needs courage. This book has been written to provide courage to teachers during their encounters with an often intimidating area of professional practice: art education. Teaching art can induce anxiety in even the most courageous of educators; therefore, the suggestions in this book should be considered analogous to the advice dispensed to the ancient Greeks by Apollo's priestesses at Delphi:

The counsels of Delphi were not advice in the strict sense,
but rather were stimulants to the individual and to the group to look inward,
to consult their own intuition and wisdom.
The oracles put the problem in a new context
so that it could be seen in a different way,
a way in which new and as of yet unimagined possibilities would become evident.[2]
Rollo May

---

[1]   Fehr, D. (1994). Promise and paradox: Art education in the postmodern
       arena. *Studies in Art Education, 35*(4), p. 216.

[2]   May, R. (1975). *The courage to create*, p. 127.

FORMAT FEATURES

This book has been designed to provide the reader with a friendly introduction to art education. I have consistently tried to present concepts and principles using language that is both concise and precise.

Content
The content has been organized into **20 topics** of particular relevance to the design and implementation of art curricula. In addition, **4 teacher guides** have been prepared to complement the colour plates.

Layout
The book has been formatted on the basis of paired **facing pages**. On most pages **information windows** appear on the left and right margins. Key words appear in **boldface**.

Icons
Blocks of information within this book have been graphically coded using the following icons:

 PRACTICE   **THEORY**   **RESEARCH**

References
Academic references have not been embedded within the text itself, however, they can be readily accessed through the **RESEARCH** information windows. APA formatting has been used consistently.

Plates
The four colour plates have been placed in the middle of this book so that they can be easily removed. The colour reproductions on the front and back covers would still be available for referencing, as well as the small black & white prints in the teacher guides. ■

RESEARCH

ART EDUCATION PERIODICALS

- **Provincial**
  BCTA Journal for Art Teachers
  Journal of the Ontario Society for Education
    through Art
  NSCAD Papers in Art Education

- **Canadian**
  Canadian Review of Art Education
  Journal of the Canadian Society for
    Education through Art
  Viewpoints

- **United States**
  Art Education
  Arts & Activities
  Journal of Aesthetic Education
  Journal of Multi-cultural and Cross-cultural
    Research in Art Education
  NAEA News
  School Arts
  Studies in Art Education

- **International**
  InSEA News

PRACTICE

A RATIONALE FOR TEACHING ART

Why should art be taught in our schools?

- **Pedagogic Value**
  Speaking personally I do not believe that art should be taught in order to display pretty pictures in school corridors or to pacify children on rainy afternoons.

  The pedagogic value of art education in schools lies in the positing of activities that challenge students to **cope with ambiguity**, **experience nuance**, and **weigh alternative courses of action**. Art provides a critical balance to other subjects which stress universal laws, correct responses, or discrete solutions.

- **Divergent Nature**
  Authentic art activities are essentially divergent both in purpose and in design. They stand in contrast to the convergent approaches used within empirical subjects like science and mathematics.

  It is possible to teach art through convergent activities by using teacher-prepared projects or by emphasizing historical and technical facts, but such strategies do not allow art students or teachers to access the existentially rich experiences that art education offers.

TOPIC 1
THE ART STUDIO

Many educators mistakenly see art rooms as noisy, chaotic, unruly, unfocused, and very messy. The root cause of such misconceptions is a lack of understanding of what *studio* really means. Studio is not just an art classroom; studio also refers to a method of nondirective teaching. Studio is an *activity* as well as a *place*.

STUDIO AS A METHOD OF NONDIRECTIVE TEACHING

Students involved in art projects are continually confronted with choices that need **personal resolution**: "*Is this line too bold? Should a symmetrical design be used in this sculpture? Does my pen & ink drawing need a coloured wash?*" and so on. Within the operation of a working studio environment, resolutions to such issues are primarily left up to each student who will decide on his/her own which approach is best.

Sometimes, however, students remain uncertain as to which course of action to take and feel the need to seek out advice. Again, within the context of a working studio environment, such **advice is typically sought from classmates**. This usually requires students to leave their own desks and walk to where others they feel can help them are sitting. In some cases, students may need to consult a number of peers at work in order to garner a wider perspective. Hence, the origin of students walking and talking that administrators are so adept at observing through the windows of studio doors. Such occurrences indicate normalcy during studio production; surprisingly to some, they also signify on-task behaviours. The so-called chaos observed in studio is actually an orderly, complex form of self- and peer instruction.

Role of the Teacher
Central to the notion of studio learning is a gradual shift in the **locus of control** away from the teacher, in whom primary control is vested during directive teaching, towards each student in the art class. This shift in locus of control should be maintained consistently from the early selection of media and subject matter straight through to the assessment of student progress (*see Topic 9: Assessing Progress*).

Is there no role for the teacher to play during nondirective teaching? Yes, actually there are several, but they are ones that some educators are unaccustomed to providing. Sometimes, the teacher acts as an **advisor**, **consultant**, **guide**, or **sounding board**; the roles fluctuate to accommodate student needs. Although art specialists sometimes have an unfortunate tendency to assume the role of master artist, art teachers rarely act in ways that parallel the role of directors or conductors in the performing arts.

THE NEED FOR PEDAGOGIC TRUST

Encouraging **student disclosure** during artistic activity (*see Topic 11: The Artist*) is a recurring theme in this book. Regardless of what form it takes, disclosure is a deeply personal act that springs from the very core of self. Even for mature adults, disclosing personal information in public can be very difficult and, once undertaken, such actions demand immediate acceptance. Should acceptance be withheld, or even slow in coming, it is very unlikely that any public disclosure will be willingly offered in the future.

As with most human emotions, **trust needs to be reciprocated**. Not only do the students need to believe that the teacher will accept whatever they choose to disclose in their art, the teacher also needs to believe that the students will act responsibly with the freedom that has been granted to them. The non-directive pedagogies required for nurturing student disclosure demand a level of trust in students that some teachers find difficult to muster, however, the failure to trust students and the retention of overt control at the teacher's desk suffocate the studio dynamics needed to spark personal disclosures in art.

TEACHERS AS PARENTS

The nurturing of artistic disclosure requires teachers to develop relationships with their students that closely parallel those between parents and their children. The degree of intervention by parents in the lives of their children steadily declines as adolescents are given increasingly greater opportunities to explore and express their senses of self. Although parents understand that this inevitable process of personal maturation necessitates a gradual change in their custodial role, they frequently find its reality difficult to accept. The tendencies to belittle adolescent attempts at mastering new tasks, to impose adult standards of behaviour, and to resent signs of developing independence are pitfalls that parents can all identify with. The greatest impediment to the healthy development of children, however, is the parental impulse to shield them from failure by directly intervening in the making of critical decisions.

Similarly, the nurturance of artistic disclosure requires a gradual reduction in the degree to which teachers directly intervene during artistic activities. Sensing the **appropriate degree of withdrawal** may be difficult for teachers with little or no familiarity with art, however, the professional observation of studio interactions and dynamics, coupled with the acquisition of experience over time, will help every classroom teacher develop an appropriate repertoire of nondirective teaching strategies. ∎

RESEARCH

THE ART STUDIO

- Courtney, R. (1989). *Play, drama & thought: The intellectual background to dramatic education* (4th ed.). Toronto, ON: Simon & Pierre.

- Hurwitz, A. (1983). *The gifted and talented in art: A guide to program planning.* Worcester, MA: Davis.

- May, R. (1975). *The courage to create.* New York, NY: W.W. Norton.

- Qualley, C. (1986). *Safety in the artroom.* Worcester, MA: Davis.

- Susi, F. (1995). *Student behaviour in art classrooms: The dynamics of discipline.* Reston, VA: National Art Education Association.

- Van Manen, M. (1991). *The tact of teaching: The meaning of pedagogical thoughtfulness.* London, ON: Althouse Press.

PRACTICE

PEDAGOGIC CONSIDERATIONS

Regardless of which developmental model art teachers decide to use, the following pedagogic principles need to be carefully considered:

- **Children are Not Miniature Adults**
  Children respond to the physical world differently than adults due to differences In their respective levels of physical, emotional, and cognitive maturation. Similarly, child art is not a crude facsimile of adult art; it represents a unique response to the physical world.

- **The Nature of Art Development**
  Although research has proven the existence of an overall progression in art development, it is neither linear nor segmental. Art development typically unfolds as a continuous but erratic exploration of media techniques and compositional arrangements.

- **Factors Affecting Art Development**
  Art development can be negatively affected by poor physical health, limited exposure to art in the home or at school, repressive cultural conditioning, and introverted personal temperament. Art development can be positively affected by reverse conditions.

TOPIC 2
ART DEVELOPMENT

All young children love to participate in art activities, however, by the end of elementary school their creative spark has usually been completely extinguished. What happens to the art development of young artists in school? What can teachers do to address this well-documented phenomenon? To answer these basic questions we need to take a look at contemporary models of art development.

ART & DEVELOPMENTAL PSYCHOLOGY

For most of this century, art has maintained its curricular status in elementary schools due to research which suggests that art activities facilitate **physiological**, **emotional**, and **cognitive child development** (*see Topic 4: Art Curricula*). While developmental psychologists have not generally been noted for their expertise as classroom teachers or practising artists their impact upon art education has been immense. In particular, Viktor Lowenfeld's Piagetian stage model of art development has provided the curricular foundation for *baby boomer* art activities across the continent since the end of the Second World War.

Scribbling	ages 2 - 4
Pre-Schematic	ages 4 - 7
Schematic	ages 7 - 9
Gang Age	ages 9 - 12
Dawning Realism	ages 12 - 14

2.1
ART DEVELOPMENT
Lowenfeld Model

INSTRUCTION & STAGE MODELS

Developmental stage models are never supposed to be rigidly applied, especially when human beings are involved. Nonetheless, in recent years a few university-based, art education researchers have made unsubstantiated claims that stage models are inherently inflexible and incapable of accommodating the frequently erratic and highly individualized nature of child art development. For teachers more familiar with children and basic classroom instruction, however, the various stage models found in virtually all current teaching methods texts continue to provide sound bases for planning elementary art activities.

2.2
TODD
I am Swimming in the Pool
Tempera on paper
45.5 x 61 cm.
Collection of J.H. Martin

ART DEVELOPMENT

- Gardner, H. (1990). *Art education and human development.* Los Angeles, CA: Getty Center for Education in the Arts.

- Irwin, R., & Grauer, K. (Eds.). (1997). *Readings in Canadian art teacher education.* Boucherville, PQ: Canadian Society for Education through Art.

- Kellogg, R. (1969). *Analyzing children's art.* Palo Alto, CA: National Press Books.

- Lowenfeld, V., & Brittain, W. (1987). *Creative and mental growth* (8th ed.). London, UK: Macmillan.

- Thompson, C. (Ed.). (1995). *The visual arts and early childhood learning.* Reston, VA: National Art Education Association.

Teaching Methods Texts
In addition to these references all of the teaching methods texts listed on page 27 have chapters which highlight models and illustrative exemplars of art development.

THE BIG CHILL

The decline in student enthusiasm for art activities usually becomes quite noticeable by grades 5 or 6:
- art typically lacks the spontaneity adored by early childhood teachers and parents
- students frequently leave their art incomplete and sometimes destroy finished art
- students become unwilling to have their art publicly critiqued or displayed
- students become frustrated over their limited success in acquiring realistic studio skills.

This developmental regression can only be addressed when teachers recognize that adolescent students are no longer children and, correspondingly, that adolescent art is substantively different than early and late forms of childhood art. *Peter Pan* has grown up. ■

CONSTRUCTING A MODE CONTINUUM

The distinctions between childhood art, adolescent art, and adult art become progressively clearer as they are discussed among practitioners and as they are discussed between the teacher and the becoming artist. When this kind of discourse becomes habit, practitioners are commensurably able to perceive their students as expressive people who are on a developmental continuum as makers and appreciators of art.[1]

ART DEVELOPMENT AS A CONTINUUM

Thus, there are two keys to maintaining life-long participation in art:
- distinguishing **childhood**, **adolescent**, and **adult art**
- celebrating each as part of a **developmental continuum**.

The field of art education has historically failed to do either of these tasks. The literature offers many curricular resources for childhood and adult art but makes few references to the transitional role played by adolescent art. Art researchers frequently lament the advent of adolescent art and concoct truly destructive theories in futile attempts to extend child art indefinitely.

In constructing a developmental continuum which respects the integrity of toddlers, children, and adolescents as young artists, our attention will be focused on the **primary mode of expression** used by each.

Adults use all of the developmental modes nurtured in early childhood art, late childhood art, and adolescent art (*see Topic 12: Styles of Expression*). **Surrealistic**, **realistic**, **abstract**, and **non-objective expressions of reality** are constructed from what adult artists *feel*, *know*, and *see*.

---

1   Retallack-Lambert, N. (1997). The world of adolescent art. In R. Irwin & K. Grauer (Eds.), *Readings in Canadian art teacher education*, p. 189.

SENSORY MODE: What Artists FEEL

Early Childhood Art
Pre-School Years

Learner Characteristics
Art development begins before the start of formal schooling as toddlers begin to explore the physical world. In the **sensory mode** young artists rely on external stimuli such as moving objects, noises, colours, and textures for creative inspiration. They discover that external stimuli can be *captured* by manipulating art media such as crayons, play dough, sand, and paint.

Developmental Progression
The sensory mode typically involves 3 levels of developmental progression. Initially, sensory art is **uncontrolled**; toddlers use gross motor skills to make random marks that remain unnamed and unrelated to visual images. Over time, however, increased motor **control** facilitates the production of more fully-formed shapes and lines. The final level involves the **naming** of art and the correlation of shapes and lines to ideas, objects, and people (*see page 12 for a sensory art exemplar*).

Instructional Strategies
Teachers need to provide toddlers with frequent and varied opportunities to express their feelings about the physical world through artistic media. Young children seldom need any extrinsic motivation at this point in their art development. Teachers simply need to allow toddlers to work without distractions, at their own rate, within a playful, accepting environment.

CONTINUUM
. . . .

EXPERIENTIAL MODE: What Artists KNOW

Late Childhood Art
Primary-Junior Grades

Learner Characteristics
Upon entering elementary school, children's exposure to the physical world expands significantly. Increased contacts with adults, other children, and new surroundings prompt an egocentric, **experiential mode** of expression. Experiential art relies on events remembered rather than objects viewed.

Developmental Progression
The experiential mode incorporates 2 levels of developmental progression. **Early symbolic** art witnesses the development of geometric shapes which evolve into recognizable people, animals, and buildings. Colours are used to convey emotions. Pictures lack any sense of depth or size relationships. **Late symbolic** art relies on more conventional uses of picture space; base lines appear for the ground and sky, for example. Since experiential art is focused on remembered images, objects unknown to children are omitted. The pictorial constraints imposed by using single sheets of paper to tell stories result in non-adult representations such as **multiple-view**, **x-ray**, and **serial** drawings (*see pages 12 & 13 for experiential art exemplars*).

Instructional Strategies
Teachers need to continue providing children with frequent opportunities to express themselves artistically. Motivation may be increased by linking art to activities that the children have directly experienced. Children may be reluctant to join group activities. Teachers should never *correct* children when they rely on multiple-view, x-ray, or serial representations in their art.

VISUAL MODE: What Artists SEE

Adolescent Art
Intermediate-Senior Grades

Learner Characteristics
By late elementary school, adolescents have reached a relatively high level of social awareness. This awareness often produces very intense studio activity especially when students can self-identify with the subject matter. On the other hand, this high level of social awareness frequently inhibits peer interactions and unduly increases levels of self-criticism.

Developmental Progression
The visual mode normally results in excessive student preoccupation with realism. Adolescent artists struggle to acquire studio techniques such as linear/aerial perspective, figure drawing, and spatial depth. Assignments which the students perceive to be juvenile can spark antisocial reactions. Visual art which involves still life, landscape, portraiture, or drawing from a live model is well-received. Student attention to detail can be extreme.

Instructional Strategies
It is critical that teachers acknowledge the growing maturity of adolescent students. Failure to provide age-appropriate media and direct instruction can be fatal. Teachers need to understand that adolescent preoccupations with realism do not stem from stylistic preferences but from misguided assumptions that adult art is invariably realistic. The frustrations which accompany adolescent attempts to produce realistic art can be reduced by introducing students to less skill-dependent forms of artistic expression such as **surrealistic**, **abstract**, and **non-objective art**. ■

ADULT ART →

TODD'S GALLERY

2.3   **SENSORY MODE**
TODD   CONTROLLED
It's a Design

In this early painting Todd has clearly attained a moderately high level of motor control. For example, the black, outlined shapes are fully enclosed and the black spirals which appear in the upper right corner indicate that Todd is continuing to experiment with new ways to control his paint brush. While there is no sense of pictorial composition in *It's a Design*, Todd has nonetheless worked to achieve a deliberate, overall distribution of pattern. Although the title indicates that Todd has not yet linked his painted shapes to objects in the real world, he is starting to identify with his art by affixing his name. The variety and placement of colours also reinforce the design.

2.4   **EXPERIENTIAL MODE**
TODD   EARLY SYMBOLIC
I am Building a Snowman

I am Building a Snowman illustrates many characteristics of early symbolic painting. Todd has begun to use geometric shapes to show objects from the real world. Typically, Todd has used one circle to represent his entire torso even though he has used three circles to construct the snowman. While this painting has a clearly defined top/bottom orientation, Todd has not yet developed sky/ground baselines. The orange patch underneath the snowman represents Todd's first step towards achieving pictorial space. The blue and purple in the snowman have been used to represent emotions rather than actual appearance. Two variations of the sun have been used.

2.5
TODD
I am Playing in the Garden

2.6
TODD
We are Riding on a Double-Decker Bus

In this late symbolic painting Todd has painted green and blue baselines to represent the ground and the sky; since they remain far apart, however, no convincing sense of pictorial space has been achieved. Although Todd has represented himself with a more realistic human figure, he has given the plants a much larger scale to correspond to their narrative importance. While Todd has continued to show the sun in a stereotypical fashion, he has obviously spent much time and thought assigning unique colour patterns and details to the various plants. In *I am Playing in the Garden* Todd has painted details on top of background areas to convey three-dimensionality.

We are Riding on a Double-Decker Bus shows an increasing sophistication in Todd's ability to tell complicated stories using single sheets of paper. First, Todd has used an **x-ray** format to show the outside and inside of the bus simultaneously. Second, **multiple-view** perspectives have been used to show the seated children from the side and the table tops from above. Third, a **serial** element has been used to suggest that the children shown in the lower tier of the bus have subsequently climbed to the second level. Notice how Todd has ignored the parts of the bus that he had not actually seen or could not remember, and the persistence of *Mr. Sun*. ∎

PRACTICE

TYPES OF CREATIVITY IN ART

Whenever art teachers plan assignments which ask students to exhibit *creativity*, it is imperative that a clear explanation be offered as to how the term is being used within the specific assignment; otherwise, students are simply left to guess what the art teacher is really expecting them to do.

Here are 4 common types of creativity and examples of how each could be observed in art assignments:

- **Originality**
  Creating very unique objects:
  Krystle's landscape of Planet 9 was the only painting which showed a night scene.

- **Flexibility**
  Finding associations among objects:
  Olga's slide presentation demonstrated how Egyptian art is similar to child art.

- **Fluency**
  Creating many different objects:
  Juan's print contained more organic shapes than any other collagraph.

- **Elaboration**
  Adding details about objects:
  Benjamin's pastel drawing of the panda revealed a lot about the animal's habitat.

TOPIC 3
CREATIVITY

Although all of the four arts are unique subjects in terms of content, they share as a common intent the nurturing of creativity. From this truism, however, a serious misunderstanding can develop: the Renaissance merger of arts *and* sciences can be lost to the polarization of arts *versus* science. It is the spark of creativity that has allowed many great scientists to enter new realms of discovery and, similarly, great artists have historically found inspiration through scientific study and new technology.

CREATIVITY AS BEHAVIOUR

Proponents of creativity as *behaviour* have traditionally come from backgrounds in the social sciences. Their efforts to supply scientific models for artistic activity dominated much of the literature during the 1950s and 60s. Despite promising early work, behaviourists have failed to produce any conclusive models of creativity, and art educators have increasingly been drawn to experiential notions of creativity.

Group Ideation
Group ideationists studied interactions among individuals which encouraged or discouraged creative thinking. From their research two techniques were developed which are commonly used in corporate management: brainstorming and synectics. While both techniques rely upon deferred judgement as a method of creative problem-solving, **brainstorming** involves the generation of as many solutions as possible, whereas **synectics** relies on the use of analogy to put persistent problems in new perspectives.

Reductionism
The idea that complex human behaviours could be understood through the study of isolated components is known in the literature as reductionism. Typically, research in this field involved pencil & paper tests such as the *Remote Associations Tests* (R.A.T.). Links made between apparently unrelated words were considered to be signs of innate creativity which could carry over into other subject areas such as art. The most influential reductionist was E. Paul Torrance who conceptualized creativity as *task analysis*. He believed that the complex processes involved during creative acts depended upon four cognitive skills which he labeled **originality**, **flexibility**, **fluency**, and **elaboration** (*see the Practice window at left*).

Personality Assessment
Research into potential social determinants of creativity proved problematic on two counts. First, most of the studies were criticized on methodological grounds; second, the data produced were inconclusive.

CREATIVITY AS EXPERIENCE

Proponents of creativity as *experience* generally come from backgrounds in the arts. They consider creativity to be a fundamentally process- rather than product-based phenomenon, fully understood only by individuals working directly and honestly in an aesthetic environment (*see Topic 13: Looking at Art*).

Existentialism
Existentialists stress the importance of **personal integrity** during encounters with expressive media, as opposed to more traditional measures of creativity such as originality and craftsmanship. Artists often self-identify with their work to the point that evaluating their art feels just like looking in a mirror.

POSTMODERNIST INFLUENCES

The modernist concept of creativity as an intuitive leap of imagination which allows artists to depart from established traditions to produce novel forms has come under attack in recent years. For example, Sharon Bailin contends that creativity is an ordinary, rational, cognitive process that is little more than **excellent thinking and performing** in an area. Unfortunately, however, she goes on to admit that skills, rules, and logic may not tell the whole story, that there is *something more* to creativity which could be expressed as inspiration, illumination, vision, genius, or just plain imagination. So the debate continues.

PEDAGOGIC CONSIDERATIONS

After more than 20 years of teaching art, I firmly believe that everybody is capable of creative activity, not just those born with **talent**. I acknowledge that genetic and social conditions ensure that children enter school with visible proclivities and dispositions, and some display more affinity for art than others. The same is true for those who excel at arithmetic, spelling, or catching bean bags. It is the professional duty of teachers, however, to foster basic levels of competence in their students across the curriculum, not just in areas that children want to explore. Elitist notions of **artistic genius** offer convenient excuses to teachers who only want to teach the students who can create art intuitively. Although such teachers do their students a great personal disservice, they do Canadian society an even greater disservice by producing empty individuals incapable of employing art in their search for a meaningful existence. ■

CREATIVITY

- Bailin, S. (1988). *Achieving extraordinary ends: An essay on creativity.* Norwell, MA: Kluwer Academic Publishers.

- Clark, R. (1994). *Art education: A Canadian perspective.* Toronto, ON: Ontario Society for Education through Art.

- Gardner, H. (1993). *Creating minds: An anatomy of creativity as seen through the lives of Freud, Einstein, Picasso, Stravinsky, Eliot, Graham, and Ghandi.* New York, NY: Basic Books.

- Hurwitz, A. (1983). *The gifted and talented in art: A guide to program planning.* Worcester, MA: Davis.

- Lowenfeld, V., & Brittain, W. (1987). *Creative and mental growth* (8th ed.). London, UK: Macmillan.

- May, R. (1975). *The courage to create.* New York, NY: W.W. Norton.

PRACTICE

PLANNING ART CURRICULA

See also Topic 5: Lesson Planning
Topic 6: Unit Planning
Topic 7: Integrated Planning

Whether art planning is premised upon instrumentalist or essentialist models, the following components typically form the core of art curricula from K · 12.

- **Studio**
  Studio is usually focused on drawing, painting, printmaking, and sculpture. Elements of these basic studio areas have been charted on pages 18 & 19. Other areas include mixed media, film, photography, and computer graphics.

- **Art History**
  The fundamentals of art history are given in *Topic 12: Styles of Expression.* Historical overviews of surrealistic, realistic, abstract, and non-objective expressions of reality in Western art are presented on pages 46 · 49.

- **Art Criticism & Aesthetics**
  Approaches to art criticism (*determining artistic preferences*) and aesthetics (*determining artistic value*) are outlined in *Topic 13: Looking at Art* and *Topic 14: Formalism.*

TOPIC 4
ART CURRICULA

Planning art curricula involves much more than just deciding when and what to draw or paint. Teachers need to step back and contemplate which philosophical approach to art education suits their specific instructional needs for, although drawing and painting activities do form the core of most art curricula, the pedagogic intent and content may vary widely from classroom to classroom.

ART AS AN EMERGENT SCHOOL SUBJECT

Art, as we know it today, did not exist in the curricula of **common schools** in the 1800s. The forerunner of contemporary art education was **drawing**, designed to train draughtsmen in mechanical illustration. Canadians may take pride in the fact that drawing was made compulsory in British North America almost a quarter century prior to the *Massachusetts Act of 1870*. It is worth noting, however, that while all common school subjects were compulsory they were given unequal status. In Ontario, for example, Egerton Ryerson divided common school subjects into *cardinal*, *required*, and *other*. The inferior status that art education continues to bear can be traced to the placement of drawing in the category of *other*.

With the gradual extension of higher grades, a new form of schooling emerged called **superior education**. For boys, superior education consisted of studies intended to provide future civic leaders with a liberal arts perspective. Drawing was retained as a *practical* subject alongside bookkeeping and commercial arithmetic. For girls, superior education consisted of studies intended to provide the wives of future civic leaders with a similar liberal arts outlook, softened by gender-specific instruction in needlework, French, modern languages, piano, dance, drawing, and painting. Since this *accomplishments curriculum* was taught in collegiate institutes, while drawing was offered in technical schools, art at the secondary school level quickly became divided into 2 streams: academic courses called **art** or **visual arts** and technical studies called **vocational art** or **graphics** · distinctions which still hobble art education today.

By the First World War, drawing courses at the elementary level had been replaced by curricula inspired by John Dewey's curricular model of active learning, Maria Montessori's pedagogic model of auto-education, and Jean Piaget's psychological model of cognitive development. Initially, elementary art activities emphasized ornamental design · a major departure from drawing's emphasis upon tedious copy books and geometric exercises. After the Second World War, elementary art underwent an even more radical transformation, emerging as a **cross-disciplinary pedagogic methodology** valued for its role in the achievement of generic educational goals rather than the attainment of artistic skills *per se*.

PHILOSOPHICAL APPROACHES TO ART EDUCATION

Instrumentalism

Instrumentalists maintain that art should be part of school curricula not so much for its innate value, but because art facilitates the acquisition of generic objectives such as **motor control**, **co-operative work habits**, **visual perceptiveness**, and **psychological well-being**. For example, John Dewey's laboratory school at the University of Chicago included both fine- and applied art activities, but they were taught within the context of child-centred themes rather than as discrete components of art education. In recent years, critical theorists have suggested that instrumental art curricula help to camouflage the competitive nature of schooling and the marginalization of student minorities by class, gender, and race. In the literature, instrumentalism is more commonly referred to as **education** *through* **art**, a term coined by Herbert Read (1943) in his futurist text *Education Through Art* in which art promotes social harmony.

Essentialism

Rather than rationalizing the contributions made by art to general education in terms of its role in the acquisition of generic skills, psychological health, or social harmony, essentialists maintain that art has inherent value as a discrete school subject. In the mid-1960s, American university scholars such as David Ecker and Manuel Barkan put forward the essentialist propositions that:

- artistic activity was a form of *qualitative problem-solving*
- the discipline consisted of 3 modes of *scientific inquiry*: **studio**, **art history**, and **art criticism**.

By the 1980s, essentialist models of discipline-based art education (DBAE) experienced a revival due to the immense financial sponsorship and political advocacy provided by the Getty Center for Education in the Arts. In the literature, essentialism is more prevalently referred to as **education** *in* **art**, or *DBAE*.

Two Sides of the Same Coin

Although instrumentalists maintain that their curricular approach is pedagogically appropriate for art students from K - 12, curricula based upon education *through* art have been adopted predominately by elementary school generalists. Similarly, although essentialists contend that their approach is also appropriate for art students from K - 12, curricula based upon education *in* art have been favoured mostly by secondary school art specialists. The result has been a critical and chronic disjuncture in art education that still awaits resolution as we enter a new century. Hopefully, the day will come when art teachers understand that instrumentalism and essentialism are really two sides of the same coin. ■

HISTORY OF ART EDUCATION

- Arnheim, R. (1989). *Thoughts on art education.* Los Angeles, CA: Getty Center for Education in the Arts.

- Clark, R. (1994). *Art education: A Canadian perspective.* Toronto, ON: Ontario Society for Education through Art.

- Efland, A. (1990). *A history of art education: Intellectual and social currents in teaching the visual arts.* New York, NY: Teachers College Press.

- Irwin, R., & Grauer, K. (Eds.). (1997). *Readings in Canadian art teacher education.* Boucherville, PQ: Canadian Society for Education through Art.

- MacGregor, R. (Ed.). (1984). *Readings in Canadian art education.* Vancouver, BC: Pacific Education Press.

- Smith, P. (1996). *The history of art education: Learning about art in American schools.* Westport, CT: Greenwood.

- Soucy, D., & Stankiewicz, M. (Eds.). (1990). *Framing the past: Essays on art education.* Reston, VA: National Art Education Association.

BASIC STUDIO PLANNING

DRAWING

MATERIALS

Mediums
- ❑ graphite pencil
- ❑ coloured pencil
- ❑ conté stick
- ❑ dust pastel
- ❑ oil pastel
- ❑ wax crayon
- ❑ India ink
- ❑ felt marker
- ❑ coloured ink

Papers
- ❑ newsprint
- ❑ manila
- ❑ cartridge
- ❑ tag
- ❑ Mayfair cover
- ❑ bristol board
- ❑ construction
- ❑ mural
- ❑ tracing

Equipment
- ❑ scissors
- ❑ x-acto knife
- ❑ compass
- ❑ glue stick
- ❑ rubber cement
- ❑ white resin
- ❑ vinyl eraser
- ❑ art gum eraser
- ❑ steel-edge ruler

TECHNIQUES

- ❑ outline
- ❑ contour
- ❑ value/tone
- ❑ stipple
- ❑ hatch
- ❑ cross-hatch

CATEGORIES

- ❑ landscape
- ❑ still life
- ❑ illustration
- ❑ portraiture
- ❑ caricature
- ❑ figure
- ❑ gesture · outline
- ❑ gesture · wire
- ❑ gesture · geometric

PAINTING

MATERIALS

Mediums
- ❑ finger paint
- ❑ coloured ink
- ❑ tempera
- ❑ gouache
- ❑ acrylic
- ❑ watercolour

Papers & Boards
- ❑ manila
- ❑ watercolour
- ❑ mural
- ❑ rice
- ❑ canvas
- ❑ masonite

Brushes
- ❑ poster
- ❑ detail
- ❑ watercolour

Equipment
- ❑ mixing palette
- ❑ paint tray
- ❑ smock
- ❑ newspaper
- ❑ water container
- ❑ paper towels

TECHNIQUES

- ❑ wash
- ❑ dry brush
- ❑ pen & ink
- ❑ wet on wet
- ❑ wet on dry
- ❑ wax resist
- ❑ dry on dry
- ❑ dry on wet
- ❑ rubber resist

CATEGORIES

- ❑ landscape
- ❑ still life
- ❑ portrait
- ❑ figure
- ❑ illustration
- ❑ graphic design

PRINTMAKING

MATERIALS

Mediums
- ❏ printing ink
- ❏ fabric ink
- ❏ stamp pads

Plates
- ❏ linoleum
- ❏ wood
- ❏ wax
- ❏ styrofoam
- ❏ plexiglass
- ❏ copper
- ❏ silk/nylon mesh
- ❏ paper/card
- ❏ masonite

Paper
- ❏ cartridge
- ❏ print
- ❏ fabric

Equipment
- ❏ linoleum cutters
- ❏ wood chisels
- ❏ stylus
- ❏ brayer
- ❏ silkscreen
- ❏ squeegee
- ❏ block press
- ❏ etching press
- ❏ scissors
- ❏ x-acto knife
- ❏ white resin glue
- ❏ inking tray

CATEGORIES

- ❏ monoprint
- ❏ stencil
- ❏ silkscreen
- ❏ relief
- ❏ rubbing
- ❏ stamping
- ❏ intaglio
- ❏ etching
- ❏ collagraph

SCULPTURE

MATERIALS

Mediums
- ❏ dough
- ❏ plasticine
- ❏ sand
- ❏ clay
- ❏ pipe cleaners
- ❏ wire
- ❏ plaster
- ❏ wood
- ❏ paper
- ❏ cardboard
- ❏ packaging
- ❏ found objects
- ❏ plexiglass
- ❏ styrofoam
- ❏ foam
- ❏ fabric
- ❏ glazes
- ❏ acrylic paints

Equipment
- ❏ modeling tools
- ❏ carving tools
- ❏ knife
- ❏ sponges
- ❏ batt
- ❏ newspaper
- ❏ plastic bag
- ❏ scissors
- ❏ wire cutters
- ❏ stapling gun
- ❏ glue
- ❏ glue gun
- ❏ plaster mould
- ❏ electric kiln
- ❏ potter's wheel

CATEGORIES

- ❏ pinch
- ❏ slab
- ❏ coil
- ❏ bas relief
- ❏ block carving
- ❏ papier mâché
- ❏ armature
- ❏ puppet
- ❏ mould
- ❏ wheelwork
- ❏ mobile
- ❏ stabile
- ❏ soft sculpture
- ❏ diorama
- ❏ installation

STUDIO TECHNIQUES & LESSON IDEAS can be researched in the elementary texts on page 21 and the teaching methods texts on page 27. ■

PRACTICE

PLANNING TIPS

- **Reducing Preparation Time**
  You can save valuable preparation time by developing planning and assignment templates with standardized headings and blocks.

- **Assigning Time Allowances**
  Many teachers assign a time allowance for each part of a lesson. While this is a helpful exercise to undergo during the planning phase, these schedules should not be rigidly adhered to during actual instruction. The timing and duration of student interactions during an art lesson are difficult to predict and usually need to be addressed right away.

- **Using Your Time and Energy Wisely**
  Assignment plans should be kept in student art journals for reference as studio work progresses. This will save you from having to repeat basic assignment information over and over. You will be able to spend your time and energy monitoring the class more productively.

- **The Map is Not the Territory**
  Lesson plans are prepared in order to guide, not regulate, instruction. Always remember to be flexible!

TOPIC 5
LESSON PLANNING

The key to building any effective curriculum is careful lesson planning. Whether the art curriculum is philosophically essentialist or instrumentalist (*see Topic 4: Art Curricula*), art teachers need to provide direct instruction on a regular basis. Since the basic principles of classroom instruction are not subject-specific, art lesson plans are not very different from those used in other subject areas.

I have seen a wide variety of formats over the years, however, and have come to the conclusion that art teachers need to separate lesson plans from assignment plans. One reason for this is simply space - it is difficult to fit lessons and assignments onto one sheet of paper. Separating these two plans also provides a level of flexibility from year to year since assignments are not linked to any specific lesson. Curricular *rigor mortis* can set in pretty quickly so avoid practices which make changing plans difficult.

PLANNING TEMPLATES

Preparing Plans
The best lesson plan that you can find is usually one that you have prepared yourself. Why is this true? Lesson plans prepared by a commercial publishing house or by a ministry of education lack important pedagogic specifics related to **teacher**, **learner**, and **physical setting** such as:
- What level of art expertise does the teacher bring to the lesson?
- What previous art experiences can the students draw upon for completing the assignment?
- How well-equipped is the classroom for facilitating the studio activity?

Since only YOU can answer these critically important questions, externally prepared lesson plans are simply unable to provide you with the most appropriate strategies for developing your own art curricula. So, while you may initiate your lesson planning by researching instructional ideas from some of the art textbooks currently available, you will always need to adapt what you find to suit your own situation.

Illustrative Plans
Nonetheless, I have prepared two basic templates so that planning for art will not appear so mysterious. These templates appear on pages 22 & 23 and should look pretty familiar to anybody who is a teacher. On pages 24 & 25 they reappear as illustrative plans for a lesson and an assignment in figure drawing. What does *11.D.3* mean? It is just a simple planning code that I devised for the easy identification of this particular lesson within the overall course of study: 11.D.3 is the third drawing lesson in grade 11.

LESSON PLAN

Degree of Detail

The degree of detail needed in a lesson plan depends upon the level of experience of the teacher who is expected to use it. For example, experienced teachers who have an extensive background in studio and art history can usually manage with notations in the margin of a day planner or attendance register. At the other extreme, novice teachers with little or no background in art usually require multiple-page, step-by-step booklets. Somewhere In the middle would be lesson plans intended for use by occasional teachers or for inspection by school administrators and parent councils. The lesson plan template presented on page 22 was designed to provide a moderate degree of detail. Although the suggested headings will likely suit most teaching situations, the spaces assigned for each planning block will probably need some adjustment.

Student Use

Lesson plans are generally not intended to be used or even seen by students, however, while teaching at the secondary school level I found them to be very helpful in getting absentee students caught up. Since our school operated on short, 40-minute periods I could devote very little time away from the rest of the class to work with these students. So, I gave all of the returning students a copy of my lesson plans and asked them to begin going over the material on their own. Later, during a relatively brief student/teacher conference, I was able to answer any questions that remained. This simple teaching strategy not only helped me cope with the short periods, it also helped reduce the number of student absences since missing an art class meant catching up largely on your own.

ASSIGNMENT PLAN

The assignment plan template shown on page 23 was intended to make studio design more concrete for **visual learners**. By sketching at the outset what their assignments might look like when completed, visual learners could obtain the confidence to translate ideas into reality. It is very important, however, that students understand that working in the art studio is rarely a linear process. Preliminary designs are almost always changed as a result of new ideas, unexpected difficulties, and constructive criticism. Equally important is the need for art teachers to ensure that **planned studio** activities are balanced with spontaneous or **emergent studio** experiences in order to model different ways of producing art. ∎

ART TEXTBOOKS

Elementary Resources

Each of the following textbook series offers detailed lessons for elementary school art. Discipline-based art education provides the curricular philosophy in most cases. The textbooks are lavishly illustrated and include large, poster reproductions of art exemplars. The *Teaching Art* kits also offer art flash cards and games.

- Brière, M. (1992). *Art image* (1-8). Montréal, PQ: Art Image Publications.

- _____. (1992). *L'image de l'art*. Montréal, PQ: Art Image Publications.

- Chapman, L. (1987). *Discover art* (1-6) (rev. ed.). Worcester, MA: Davis.

- _____. (1989). *Teaching art: Grades 1-3.* Worcester, MA: Davis.

- _____. (1989). *Teaching art: Grades 4-6.* Worcester, MA: Davis.

- Hubbard, G. (1987). *Art in action* (1-8). San Diego, CA: Coronado.

- Thompson, C. (1994). *Art image preschool* (series). Montréal, PQ: Art Image Publications.

RESEARCH

LESSON PREPARATION

- Instructional Aids

- Reference Texts

- Art Exemplars

LESSON PLAN

LESSON TITLE

Outcomes

Introduction

Development

Application

ASSIGNMENT PLAN

ASSIGNMENT TITLE

PRACTICE

ASSIGNMENT INFORMATION

- Description

- Time

- Media

- Size

- Materials

- Assessment

RESEARCH

LESSON PREPARATION

- **Instructional Aids**
  student model
  chair
  spotlight

- **Reference Texts**
  Library texts on Leonardo da Vinci
  as available

- **Art Exemplars**
  Plate 2
  DENNIS BURTON. *Newark, New Jersey, July 11 1967 or Across the Peace Bridge* 1968
  (*see Guide 2: Gallery 2 on pages 74 & 75*)

LESSON PLAN   11.D.3
FIGURE DRAWING

WORKING SKETCHES

Outcomes
Students will:
- complete working sketches of the human figure from front and side views
- demonstrate an understanding of proper body proportions
- apply appropriate shading using a complete range of value.

Introduction
The lesson will begin with a review of some gesture drawings completed during a previous lesson.

Working sketches by Leonardo da Vinci, intended as guides for more extended figure drawing, will be shown.

Development
Strategies for achieving accurate body proportions will be reviewed such as:
- using a pencil to visually estimate relative size relationships between parts of the body
- using the head as a standard unit of measure with an adult figure having 8 **heads** as follows:
  crown   chin   nipple   navel   crotch   mid-thigh   kneecap   calf   sole.

The concept of **foreshortening** will be illustrated through reference to *Newark, New Jersey, July 11 1967 or Across the Peace Bridge* 1968 by Dennis Burton (*see Gallery 2 pages 74 & 75*).

With the assistance of a student model 2 working sketches will be completed, one from a front view and the other from a side view.

The direction of the light source will be noted and appropriate shading added to each of the sketches.

Application
Students will complete a series of front and side view working sketches.

Sufficient detail and attention to shading for use as guides for extended figure drawing will be stressed.

ASSIGNMENT PLAN 11.D.3
FIGURE DRAWING

EXTENDED DRAWING

5.1
ROGER CLARK
Seated Nude Wearing Boots 1987
Graphite on paper
45.5 x 61 cm.
Collection of the artist

ASSIGNMENT INFORMATION

- **Description**
  An extended figure drawing with proper body proportions will be completed.

  A full range of value must be demonstrated using a 7-segment graduated value strip.

- **Time**   6 x 75 minutes

- **Media**   graphite on paper

- **Size**   45.5 x 61 cm.

- **Materials**
  working sketches - front or side view
  Mayfair cover paper - white
  graphite pencils - 2H, 2B, 4B
  vinyl eraser
  spray fixative

- **Assessment**
  30 %   complexity and effort
  30 %   accuracy of proportion
  30 %   application of value
  10 %   likeness to model/sketch

PRACTICE

THRESHOLDS OF TOLERANCE

When planning curricula, teachers need to be conscious of their personal thresholds of pedagogic tolerance in these areas:

- **Noise**
  Can you cope with students talking in the studio while music is being played?

- **Space**
  How comfortable are you teaching or monitoring students at their tables?

- **Size of Group**
  Do you prefer to work with students in small groups or as an entire class?

- **Decision-Making**
  Do you encourage students to resolve studio issues themselves or with peers?

- **Teacher Interests**
  Do your own personal preferences take precedence over student interests?

- **Evaluation & Standards**
  What role do students play in the evaluation of art assignments?

- **Teacher Role**
  How do you want students to think of you? How do you gain their respect?

TOPIC 6
UNIT PLANNING

Effective art curricula do not consist of occasional painting activities on rainy, Friday afternoons. Curriculum planning is one of the most important pedagogic tasks that teachers are responsible for undertaking whether by themselves or as part of school-based curriculum writing teams. While courses of study are often set by art consultants, unit plans are usually prepared by classroom teachers.

SEQUENCE & COMPONENTS

The planning sequence begins with a short **rationale** which explains why this particular material has been selected for instruction. This is followed by an analysis of the **physical setting** in which the unit will be implemented. Attention is focused upon factors which directly affect the intended instruction, such as a lack of sinks or drying racks, previous teacher or student experiences with clay, and so forth. The identified **learning outcomes** (2 - 3) should be limited to those specifically related to the unit; more general expectations such as co-operative work habits are usually covered in overall courses of study. **Lesson plans** (2 - 5) need to have a common curricular strand otherwise they remain isolated lessons rather than a cohesive unit. Strands may be selected from any of the curricular components listed in table 6.2. Typically, studio strands involve media, composition, or theme. For example, a unit which includes lessons on origami, puppets, and clay pipes has media (i.e., sculpture) as its curricular strand. Teachers are urged to leave at least 1 of media, composition, or theme open so that students are able to personalize their work. Detailed **assessment procedures** should be made clear to students before any assignments are begun. Student roles, such as maintaining studio journals, should be emphasized.

6.1
UNIT PLANNING
Sequence

Rationale	provide curricular reasons why the students should learn this particular material
Setting	list relevant characteristics of the school, classroom, students, and teacher
Outcomes	describe what the students will know or be able to do when the unit is over
Lessons	plan 2 or more activities which will help the students achieve these outcomes
Assessment	explain how student progress will be assessed both formatively and summatively

Studio				Art History	Art Criticism
Media	Composition		Theme		
	Elements	*Principles*		chronological	description
				monumental	analysis
drawing	line	unity		biographical	interpretation
painting	shape	balance		thematic	judgement
printmaking	colour	contrast		experiential	
sculpture	value	emphasis			**Aesthetics**
film	texture	movement			
computers					experiential
photography					response
mixed media					

6.2
UNIT PLANNING
Components

PEDAGOGIC CONSIDERATIONS

It is my belief that art teachers have traditionally over-emphasized the importance of studio activities at the expense of art history, art criticism, and aesthetics. I hope that this introduction to art education will provide the field with a broader conception of the subject so that **production** and **appreciation** will receive more equal treatment in our schools. All of the teaching methods texts in the Research window, as well as the elementary texts found on page 21, provide examples of this curricular balance.

I also urge teachers to design their instructional activities so that students are encouraged to link their art assignments in school with their lived experiences at home. One of the easiest and most effective ways of achieving this goal is allowing students to provide their own **subject matter** or **theme**. Leaving this element of unit planning open not only keeps art students personally motivated, it also promotes a greater diversity of expression and more opportunities for indirect learning in the studio. ∎

TEACHING METHODS

- Cohen, E., & Gainer, R. (1995). *Art: Another language for learning* (3 rd ed.). Portsmouth, NH: Heinemann.

- Herberholz, B., & Hanson, L. (1995). *Early childhood art* (5 th ed.). Toronto, ON: Brown & Benchmark.

- Herberholz, D., & Herberholz, B. (1998). *Artworks for elementary teachers: Developing artistic and perceptual awareness* (8 th ed.). New York, NY: McGraw Hill.

- Hurwitz, A., & Day, M. (1995). *Children and their art: Methods for the elementary school* (6 th ed.). Toronto, ON: Harcourt Brace College Publishers.

- Linderman, M. (1997). *Art in the elementary school* (5 th ed.). Toronto, ON: Brown & Benchmark.

- Wachowiak, F., & Clements, R. (1997). *Emphasis art: A qualitative art program for elementary and middle schools* (6 th ed.). Toronto, ON: Longman.

PRACTICE

ASSESSING INTEGRATED CURRICULA

Teachers can use the following evaluative criteria to assess the efficacy of teaching art through an integrated curriculum:

- **Integrity**
  Disciplinary integrity is compromised when content is presented superficially:
  Does the teacher need any art expertise?
  Do the students need any art instruction?
  Is there an art activity to be completed?

- **Authenticity**
  Each type of knowledge that subjects have to offer should find expression in integrated curricula. For art, this means incorporating the disciplines of studio, art history, art criticism, and aesthetics.

- **Diversity**
  Integration can produce its own rigidity if curricular diversity is limited:
  Is art only integrated with performing arts?
  Is thematic integration over-emphasized?
  Is art accorded equal status and time?

- **Flexibility**
  It is important not to teach art in the same way as science or mathematics:
  Are divergent activities encouraged?
  Are nondirective teaching strategies used?
  Are intuitive responses accepted?

TOPIC 7
INTEGRATED PLANNING

Curricular integration is nothing new. Effective classroom teachers everywhere, even those who are secondary school subject specialists, have always planned integrated activities for students. The current information explosion, however, has produced greater interest in integrated curricula. Even in the area of arts education, the traditional curricular emphases upon art and music have been significantly impacted by the recent introduction of drama and dance in many educational jurisdictions.

Curricular integration is not about whether subjects, which are just simplified versions of disciplines, should be combined for organizational purposes such as timetabling; rather, integration is about the efficacy of combining subjects for the purpose of **helping students acquire knowledge more efficiently**. The value of school subjects, however, is inextricably linked to debates about generalist *versus* specialist teacher preparation. As such, it is not difficult to understand why the trend towards integrated curricula has proven to be a lightning rod for heated discussions among elementary and secondary teachers.

MODELS OF CURRICULAR INTEGRATION

The idea that knowledge is not a singular entity but a grouping of disparate *types* of knowledge has been around since Aristotle organized knowledge into theoretical (*science & mathematics*), practical (*politics & ethics*), and productive (*music & architecture*). Today, we can find similar concepts expressed within Howard Gardner's **theory of multiple intelligences** which suggests at least seven different intelligences: mathematical, linguistic, musical, spatial, kinesthetic, interpersonal, and intrapersonal.

Nonetheless, curricula do not need to be planned around school subjects *per se*. One method frequently put forward as a practical way of reducing the territorial rigidity of school subjects is the **clustering** of similar disciplines. For example, elementary curricula in Ontario are clustered around four *core areas*: arts; individual and society; language; and, mathematics, science, and technology. In most Canadian provinces arts clusters consisting of art, dance, drama, and music have become generally accepted.

There are many different models of curricular integration from which to choose. Indeed, it may come as a shock to some advocates of integration to learn that traditional, subject-based curricula represent perfectly valid approaches to integration. As shown in table 7.1 types of knowledge can be integrated 3 different ways: **within disciplines**, **across disciplines**, and **within & across learners**. It is worth noting that 8 of Fogarty's 10 models presuppose the continued existence of traditional school subjects.

	Within Disciplines	
Fragmented	the traditional model of separate disciplines which fragments subjects	
Connected	within each subject content is sequenced by unit and topic from year to year	
Nested	within each subject social, cognitive, and discipline-specific skills are targeted	

Within Disciplines

Fragmented the traditional model of separate disciplines which fragments subjects
Connected within each subject content is sequenced by unit and topic from year to year
Nested within each subject social, cognitive, and discipline-specific skills are targeted

Across Disciplines

Sequenced topics or units are rearranged and taught at the same time in each subject
Shared concepts which overlap in two subjects are jointly planned and taught
Webbed a single theme is explored within a variety of subjects
Threaded metacurricular skills such as critical thinking are emphasized across subjects
Integrated this interdisciplinary model involves joint planning and teaching in many subjects

Within & Across Learners

Immersed the learner filters new knowledge through the lens of discipline-specific expertise
Networked new knowledge prompts the learner to seek out experts in a variety of disciplines

7.1
TYPES OF INTEGRATION
Fogarty Model

ART & THE PERFORMING ARTS

While all four arts subjects are unique and of equal educational value, it is important to acknowledge that art usually stands apart from the performing arts which include dance, drama, and music. Art is an indirect encounter between the subjective self and the objective world, as are literary and media arts. It is art's **lack of direct, corporeal action** that separates it from the performing arts. Artists are seldom found in galleries and we rarely see them at work in their studios. In schools, the role of the art teacher is profoundly different from the role of a director, conductor, or producer (*see Topic 1: The Art Studio*). Art teachers beware: integrated arts curricula are often just school musicals under a different billing. While musicals worked for Mickey Rooney and Judy Garland, they leave art students in the dark. ■

INTEGRATED ARTS

- Edwards, L. (1997). *The creative arts: A process approach for teachers and children* (2nd ed.). Toronto, ON: Prentice Hall.

- Fogarty, R. (1991). *How to integrate the curricula: The mindful school* (series). Palatine, IL: Skylight.

- Gardner, H. (1993). *Creating minds: An anatomy of creativity as seen through the lives of Freud, Einstein, Picasso, Stravinsky, Eliot, Graham, and Ghandi.* New York, NY: Basic Books.

- Goldberg, M. (1997). *Arts and learning: An integrated approach to teaching and learning in multicultural and multilingual settings.* Toronto, ON: Copp Clark Longman.

- Jalongo, M., & Stamp. L. (1997). *The arts in children's lives: Aesthetic education in early childhood.* Toronto, ON: Allyn and Bacon.

- Naested, I. (1998). *Art in the classroom: An integrated approach to teaching art in Canadian elementary and middle schools.* Toronto, ON: Harcourt Brace.

PRACTICE

THE SOUNDS OF SILENCE

Okay, so you've finished your art instruction and set the students to work on their new assignments - but nobody seems to be moving.

What's wrong with this picture? Nothing. The students are just taking some time to digest the material that you have taught them before deciding how to apply it in their studio assignments.

While this little scenario probably sounds pretty basic I still panic when my students don't begin producing masterpieces right after the conclusion of my lesson. I have an overwhelming urge to dash around the room and do whatever is necessary to get those pencils moving or at least prompt some signs of life.

At the root of this anxiety is the fear that I have somehow failed as a teacher and an assumption that my students will produce terrible work. At moments like these art teachers need to rely on **pedagogic trust** (*see Topic 1: The Art Studio*) and have faith in their students as well as themselves. If this sounds easy, it should be, but it isn't. Just know that you have done your best and that your students will come through with flying colours. They always do.

TOPIC 8
MONITORING PROGRESS

Not all students enjoy art. This is a taboo topic that most books on art education rarely address. Proponents of art curricula rooted in developmental psychology (*see Topic 2: Art Development*) are particularly fond of emphasizing the supposed universality of children's innate desire to express themselves through the direct manipulation of concrete materials. Virtually all art books are filled with photographs showing happy, on-task learners but every classroom teacher knows that not all students can summon the courage needed to create. In fact, some students are so frightened at the prospect of having to *perform* in art that they deliberately misbehave in order to be sent out of the room.

MOTIVATING RELUCTANT STUDENTS

There are many reasons why students might be reluctant to *get going* in art but 3 common impediments come quickly to mind: **a lack of trust**, **a lack of confidence**, and **a lack of adequate direct instruction**. These problems seem to become most problematic during *the big chill* in junior-intermediate grades. The solution, of course, is to address the learning deficits that lie at the root of each problem, that is, instilling trust, building self-confidence, and providing adequate levels of direct instruction, but these are long-term strategies that do not help teachers convince reluctant students to *get going* right away.

Teachers need to resist turning to short-term strategies such as showing students sample solutions or doing part of the art assignment for them. Although well-intentioned, motivational shortcuts actually tend to reinforce feelings of performance inadequacy by inadvertently sending the wrong message that, *"You're right, I know you can't do this work, so I'll just do it for you rather than try to teach you anything new."*

Well then, how can art teachers motivate reluctant students? The solution is to draw upon experiences, backgrounds, or skills that the students already possess, and to start building performance confidence by working with whatever the students can bring to the task at-hand. Perhaps they have worked with clay, maybe they live on a farm, or perhaps they know a lot about geometry. Take whatever the students already know and use it to **temporarily displace the unfamiliar task** that is causing such deep anxiety:
- if the **media** can be substituted with clay, then clay it is
- if the **subject matter** can be changed to a farm scene, then go for it
- if the **style** can be converted to cubism, then we're off and running.

Art curricula that are comprehensive in scope help ensure that students experience success regularly and each success helps provide anxious students with more confidence for coping with new challenges.

PEDAGOGIC CONSIDERATIONS

Using Instructional Samples
When I first started teaching secondary school art, I faithfully prepared three instructional samples for each studio project that I assigned. I had hoped to encourage the weaker students by showing them a few potential solutions but, instead, I'm afraid that I only reinforced their poor levels of self-confidence. Typically, the students produced projects that were only variations on the samples I had shown them. Even the more capable students seemed unable or unwilling to deviate from the instructional samples. In later years I received far better results when I showed samples only to the most reluctant students.

Circulating in the Studio
Once students have begun working on studio assignments, I strongly urge teachers to spend their time circulating in the studio rather than sitting at their desks expecting students to come to them for help. Don't hover over their shoulders however. Most students find such behaviour intrusive and intimidating. Instead, let students know that you are interested and available by casually walking around the studio with an air of professional confidence and approachability. I always try to spend most of my studio time near the back of the art room to compensate for all the time that I spend at the front while instructing.

Complimenting Students
In spite of all the years that I have been teaching art, I still feel awkward stopping and complimenting a student on the current assignment and then moving on. Somehow I worry that the other students nearby feel ignored or assume that their own work was not worthy of my attention, let alone my praise. On the other hand, stopping at every student's desk and offering a compliment is not only impractical but highly unconvincing. So, I advise teachers to only offer sincere compliments but to monitor their student contacts and assignments so that, over the long haul, all students receive praise for their work.

Working on Student Assignments
When circulating during studio, art teachers are very frequently asked to do part of student assignments. Working directly on student projects is **never** a good idea for a number of reasons. Often students are surprisingly ungrateful for your artistic contributions and suggest that you have ruined their entire work. Conversely, other students feel even more inadequate and become ever more dependent on your help. If and when you do decide to show students how to draw or paint, work on another sheet of paper. Portions of art completed by an adult make student assignments look worse than they really are. ■

MONITORING PROGRESS

- Courtney, R. (1989). *Play, drama & thought: The intellectual background to dramatic education* (4th ed.). Toronto, ON: Simon & Pierre.

- Hurwitz, A. (1983). *The gifted and talented in art: A guide to program planning.* Worcester, MA: Davis.

- May, R. (1975). *The courage to create.* New York, NY: W.W. Norton.

- Qualley, C. (1986). *Safety in the artroom.* Worcester, MA: Davis.

- Susi, F. (1995). *Student behavior in art classrooms: The dynamics of discipline.* Reston, VA: National Art Education Association.

- Van Manen, M. (1991). *The tact of teaching: The meaning of pedagogical thoughtfulness.* London, ON: Althouse Press.

PRACTICE

ASSESSMENT TIPS

- **Dealing With Mistakes**
  It is rarely necessary to draw student attention to mistakes. Work from the positive by highlighting works that have been done correctly. Most students are subsequently able to detect mistakes in their own work by making comparisons with the exemplars. When necessary, draw attention to mistakes in private.

- **Learning From Mistakes**
  One of the best ways to learn is by making mistakes. Acing new material is something that we all hope for, but beginner's luck can lead to superficial accomplishments that cannot be replicated. The process of recognizing and analyzing mistakes, on the other hand, increases the likelihood that we will attain authentic learning.

- **Using Student Work**
  When using student work as exemplars try to avoid identifying individuals with their art. One way to do this is to have students put their names on the reverse side of art projects. A second strategy involves using art from a previous year or from another class. A third way is to not allow individual names to be used during class discussions or critiques.

TOPIC 9
ASSESSING PROGRESS

Beyond a doubt, the most contentious part of teaching art is the assessment of student progress. Too many adults can vividly recall insensitive art teachers holding up their paintings in class as an example of what *not* to do. You might be relieved to know that happened to me in grade 7, *of course, I'm over it now ..* Quite understandably, such memories have often led classroom teachers to pledge never to subject their own students to such humiliating experiences. Unfortunately, however, such pledges have also frequently led to wholesale aversions to any form of art assessment whatsoever.

COMMON EXCUSES FOR AVOIDING ASSESSMENT

Some teachers sidestep student assessment by stressing the subjective nature of artistic expression: "*How can I evaluate somebody else's self-expression?*" Well, teachers can't - at least not by themselves. Whenever subjectivity is present in art assignments teachers need to access student comments through such assessment strategies as **self-critiques**, teacher/student **conferences**, art **journals**, and **portfolios**.

Another common way of avoiding assessment in art involves the assignment of teacher-prepared and *student proof* projects. While such art curricula result in predictable and often identical artifacts that reduce the need for individual assessment, they also reduce personal disclosure (*see Topic 11: The Artist*) to the point that art becomes little more than busywork, a curricular mirage with the facade of creativity.

Other teachers try to avoid art assessment by claiming that they stress **process** rather than **product**. Implicit in this position, of course, is the suggestion that process cannot be validly assessed on its own. Process-based art activities can, indeed, be assessed:
- by teachers through anecdotal comments or objective-specific checklists
- by students through art journals or portfolios.

Such strategies can be enriched by teacher/student conferences held as studio assignments take shape.

It should be pointed out, however, that authentic art curricula rarely separate process from product:
- How good can a process be if it does not beg for physical application?
  Not much.
- How frequently can good products result merely by chance?
  Not often.

In art education, good processes lead to good products, and good products result from good processes.

PEDAGOGIC CONSIDERATIONS

Celebrating Progress
The assessment of student progress ought to be a positive event. Surely each student has progressed, at least to some degree, as a result of the instruction and activities undertaken. Teachers need to realize that **students want to celebrate what they have accomplished**. This is especially true for art students who discover and disclose something important about themselves in each drawing, painting, print, and sculpture that they produce. Unfortunately, however, teachers tend to rush on to the next lesson and neglect to garner student comments when they are most easily elicited and readily utilized.

Most adults associate assessment with evaluation and evaluation, in turn, with negative criticism. We need to re-focus assessment processes so that they celebrate accomplishments rather than expose deficiencies. When devising assessment strategies, teachers should seek ways of finding out what students *know* or what students can *do*, not what they don't know or can't do. Although this might seem to be a mere play on semantics, it is not. Do your students begin with *0%* and work towards a passing grade or do they begin from a position of teacher confidence? Can they achieve *100%* or are there factors that keep their marks safely between *40* and *80%*? Do you word questions so that your students can demonstrate personally relevant competencies or do you design them to meet your own interests?

Reporting Progress
Reporting student progress in art is often inadequately conveyed by quantitative, norm-referenced scales such as percentages, numerical scores, or alphabetic grades. Generally speaking, art achievements are more usefully reported through qualitative, self-referenced instruments such as **anecdotal comments**, **conferences**, or **checklists**. Despite the rich mine of information offered by qualitative formats, however, administrators and parents inexplicably prefer to rely upon letters of the alphabet or two-digit numbers.

Whatever reporting format they select, teachers should avoid assigning assessments they cannot defend. For example, teachers need to be able to describe at least 3 or 4 attributes that would distinguish an *A* from a *B*; if they find this difficult to do, it would seem prudent to use some other assessment format. Teachers also need to apply common sense to norm-referenced formats such as percentages. While it is easy to devise a marking scheme that adds up to *100%* defending a mark of *74%* over *73%* is simply not possible for most art activities. Numerical intervals such as .. *70%* .. *75%* .. *80%* .. or the numbers *1* through *10* suggest less precision than percentages and allow for more defensible reporting. ∎

RESEARCH

ART ASSESSMENT

- Boughton, D. (1994). *Evaluation and assessment in visual arts education.* Geelong, Australia: Deakin University Press.

- Etobicoke Board of Education. (1987). *Making the grade: Evaluating student progress.* Toronto, ON: Prentice-Hall.

- MacGregor, R., Lemerise, S., Potts, M., & Roberts, B. (1994). *Assessment in the arts: A cross-Canada study.* Vancouver, BC: University of British Columbia.

- Peeno, L. (Ed.). (1995). *Adaptations of the national visual arts standards.* Reston, VA: National Art Education Association.

Teaching Methods Texts
In addition to these references all of the teaching methods texts listed on page 27 have chapters which highlight models and illustrative exemplars of art assessment.

ASSESSING PROCESS

PORTFOLIOS

Portfolios have traditionally been kept by artists as a way of continually improving studio techniques and as a source of new ideas and inspiration. For art teachers, however, portfolios provide a practical way of assessing student progress over the course of several weeks, months, or even years. Portfolios are especially valuable vehicles for art assessment because they allow teachers to physically trace the gradual evolution of creative thought.

PORTFOLIOS & FORMATIVE ASSESSMENT

Student art portfolios should be introduced during primary grades when children are willing to participate in art activities and talk about their work with teachers and classmates. By junior grades, art journals should be added. When operating in tandem, portfolios and journals help young artists understand how art is affected by life experiences and vice-versa. Over time, art portfolios should contain **all** of the following:
- working sketches, rough work, and research
- finished work representing a variety of media
- incomplete, damaged, and unsuccessful work.

It is impossible to assess overall student progress when portfolios contain only finished and exemplary work or fail to involve a wide variety of media.

PORTFOLIOS & SUMMATIVE ASSESSMENT

Although art portfolios are most valuable for tracking student work over time, they can of course be used as part of summative assessment as well. When using portfolios for summative assessment, I suggest that teachers allow students to select a portion of their collected works, say 4 out of 6, for marks; otherwise, students will be reluctant to keep unsuccessful work.

JOURNALS

One of the best ways to encourage life-long interest in art is the art journal. Journals help students to see art as a potential career, hobby, or lifestyle and not just simply another school subject. An art journal involves more than keeping a notebook or maintaining a sketchbook although notes and sketches are two key elements of any journal. Journals can be introduced to students in junior grades and made more complex for senior students.

COMPONENTS OF AN ART JOURNAL

- **Sketches**
  practice in studio techniques and experiments with new media

- **Notes**
  art notes and handouts, plus personal anecdotes and reminders

- **Clippings**
  newspaper columns, magazine articles, and community items

- **Images**
  photographs, advertisements, prints, and low-relief sculptures

- **Texts**
  prose, poems, short stories, diary entries, and quick thoughts

- **Memorabilia**
  ticket stubs, ribbons, dried plants, road maps, and brochures

- **Comments**
  teacher and family responses, self critiques, and peer critiques

CHECKLISTS

Checklists provide a clear and efficient way of assessing student behaviour. Ideally, art checklists should reflect a balance between behaviours related directly to art and others focused on personal development. Checklists may be completed by individual students, the teacher, or co-operatively. The following statements were prepared for junior-intermediate students; adjustments for younger and older students would need to be considered.

ART CHECKLIST

U = Usually   **S** = Sometimes   **R** = Rarely

U	S	R	
❑	❑	❑	I work as hard as I can on my assignments.
❑	❑	❑	I am courteous and helpful to my classmates.
❑	❑	❑	I take care of art supplies and equipment.
❑	❑	❑	I express something that is important to me in my art.
❑	❑	❑	I clean up my own desk and help tidy the counters.
❑	❑	❑	I keep all of my art in my portfolio.
❑	❑	❑	I contribute my fair share to group work.
❑	❑	❑	I keep notes and handouts in my journal.
❑	❑	❑	I can work by myself and ignore distractions.
❑	❑	❑	I use proper art vocabulary.
❑	❑	❑	I am willing to talk about my art.
❑	❑	❑	I listen to suggestions about my art.
❑	❑	❑	I am willing to have my art displayed.
❑	❑	❑	I help the teacher assess my art.
❑	❑	❑	I try to learn from my mistakes.
❑	❑	❑	I try to learn from my classmates.

ANECDOTES

Teachers very often assess student behaviour anecdotally in order to avoid appearing authoritarian or impersonal. Anecdotal comments are especially popular with primary-junior teachers who use them for summative as well as formative levels of assessment. It is important to include both praise and constructive criticism whenever preparing anecdotal comments for no student, or art, can be fully assessed in solely positive or negative terms.

SUPERIOR PROGRESS   Mohammed, Grade 5

Congratulations, Mohammed, on your papier mâché dragon - it looks just as real as the dinosaurs that we saw at the museum! I want to thank you for helping the other students get their projects finished in time for our Open House. I'd be glad to go over the Emily Carr CD with you again - your biography needs more details.

SATISFACTORY PROGRESS   Chloe, Grade 8

Chloe, your oil pastel landscape has really captured a sense of depth - well done! I have noticed that your portfolio is gradually getting filled with some interesting working sketches - keep adding more. Watch the clock more closely, Chloe, you still aren't giving yourself enough time to clean up your desk and store your art.

UNSATISFACTORY PROGRESS   Wolfgang, Grade 11

I am pleased to see that you are settling down this month and concentrating on your collagraph assignment - I'm sure that you will pull a fine print. Your figure drawings, however, have still not been completed. Your coil bowl was not stored properly and needs to be completely re-done. Try to talk less during class. ■

ASSESSING PRODUCT

SELF CRITIQUES

Since most authentic art assignments invite a variety of student solutions, it is important that teachers address the resulting element of subjectivity by soliciting student input as part of summative assessment procedures. I suggest that student comments be sought at the outset so that teachers do not inadvertently *read into* studio work qualities that were not intended by the artist, or unduly predispose student responses to parallel their own.

ACCESSING STUDENT COMMENTS

Regardless of whether the students are in elementary or secondary grades, there are 3 important questions that all self-critiques should address:
- What aspects of this project am I most proud of? *Why?*
- What aspects of this project am I most disappointed with? *Why?*
- What would I do differently if I were to do this project over? *Why?*

Thus, student self-critiques are initially focused upon positive, celebrative comments. Subsequently, less satisfactory results are addressed with the intention of discovering how better results could be achieved the next time. The emphasis throughout, however, remains the same: providing students with an opportunity to show what art concepts and skills they have learned - even those learned the hard way through disappointing errors or mishaps.

Self-critiques should also include some indication of what final summative assessment the students feel would be fair. Contrary to the expectations frequently held by teachers who do not ask their students to complete self-critiques, students do not suggest unreasonably high assessments very often and, when they do, teachers have a clear responsibility to explain why the suggested assessment is too high and assign a more realistic one. Students are their own worst critics, especially when art is being assessed.

CONFERENCES

Although teacher/student conferences occur on a regular basis throughout the course of teaching art, they are especially important during summative evaluation when they follow a somewhat more predictable and structured sequence of events. Conferencing with students provides teachers with especially rich opportunities for establishing, maintaining, and extending the **pedagogic trust** that nurtures studio work (*see Topic 1: The Art Studio*).

A TYPICAL SUMMATIVE CONFERENCE

Since it is unlikely that summative conferences can take place outside of regular class time, it is important that any discussion not be overheard by other students; consequently, talks held at the teacher's desk or in corners of the room are preferable to those conducted at students' desks or tables.

In most cases the conference can be undertaken with the art in-hand which is a great help especially when three-dimensional work is being assessed. In the case of older children and adolescent students, the discussion can be structured along comments outlined in self-critiques written in advance. A quick scan of such student comments at the outset can help teachers ascertain whether or not their own opinions are similar or widely divergent. Such awareness can help teachers phrase their questions more tactfully and anticipate student responses more accurately.

Ideally, conferences should prove informative for the student and teacher; both should acquire a greater understanding of the particular strengths and weaknesses of the art work under assessment. At the conclusion of the conference a mutually agreed-upon letter grade, mark, or anecdotal comment should be determined. Should agreement not be achieved even after a second conference is held the teacher's assessment should prevail.

PEER CRITIQUES

Since art students are encouraged to consult with their classmates during studio activities, it is only logical that such peer interactions should form part of summative assessment procedures, too. As frequently suggested in this book, peer critiques should be initially introduced during primary grades while the children are still willing to talk about their art and before the self-conscious **gang stage** emerges during junior-intermediate grades.

PRIMARY-JUNIOR PEER CRITIQUES

Critiquing skills can be introduced to young children through discussions held during class or group **share times**. Teachers will need to moderate discussions and model age-appropriate techniques for responding to art such as **scanning** for compositional elements like shape, line, and, colour.

JUNIOR-INTERMEDIATE PEER CRITIQUES

Older children and adolescents are often painfully shy and self-conscious; therefore, it is especially important at this stage that peer critiques stay focused solely on the art - not individuals! Responses should be related to compositional principles like balance, contrast, emphasis, and movement.

INTERMEDIATE-SENIOR PEER CRITIQUES

In secondary school grades, peer critiques are frequently linked to artists and styles of expression previously encountered in art appreciation units. After careful consideration, teachers may allow sufficiently mature senior students to direct their comments to specific individuals in the art class.

TESTS & ESSAYS

Yes, there can be wrong answers in art! Art education is not totally devoid of objective forms of knowledge or correct methods for studio production. At the outset, however, I wish to preface this discussion of tests and essays by cautioning teachers not to rely too heavily on factual approaches to art. Over-reliance upon objective content robs art students of opportunities to experience subjectivity within the safe confines of school-based learning.

TESTS IN ART EDUCATION

Since the 1980s, art curricula have concentrated less on studio production and more on art appreciation. Discipline-based art education (DBAE) in particular (*see Topic 4: Art Curricula*) envisages studio as only one of four constituent emphases along with art history, art criticism, and aesthetics; consequently, short quizzes, tests, and even examinations have received much greater attention. When I was a secondary school department head our art examinations lasted 90 minutes and consisted of three sections:
- questions related to studio techniques
- a short essay related to art appreciation
- a practical exercise which linked studio with art history.

ESSAYS IN ART EDUCATION

An unexpected result of our department's emphasis upon art appreciation was the emergence of a significant percentage of students whose primary motivation for taking secondary school art courses was no longer studio. These students realized that as future members of Canadian society they needed to develop an awareness of culture through knowledge *about* art; for them, essays and term papers facilitated such personal growth. ■

PRACTICE

SUGGESTIONS FOR ART DISPLAYS

The following suggestions are offered as practical ways of making art displays part of the learning process for participants and viewers alike:

- **Student Volunteers**
  Don't put art displays up all by yourself. Depending upon the grade level you are teaching, invite your students to get involved in framing, labeling, and hanging the art. Always remember that student displays should look age-appropriate to viewers.

- **On-Site Artists**
  Have you considered asking some of the students to act as on-site artists during the art show? It is something that they will always remember, and it will do wonders for their self-esteem. Viewers, too, will benefit by seeing the processes behind the products being exhibited.

- **Didactic Panels**
  Viewers can more fully appreciate the processes involved in making art when didactic, or explanatory, panels are placed alongside art work on display. In addition to technical information, didactic notes can also provide historical and cultural information.

TOPIC 10
DISPLAYING ART

Perhaps the best way to demonstrate artistic achievement to students, administrators, and parents is to provide frequent opportunities for displays. One of the innate strengths of art education is its ability to show physical evidence of student progress. When sensitively planned, displays facilitate the critically important, but often overlooked, celebrative element of summative assessment.

SPACE LIMITATIONS

There are several aspects to displaying student art that need to be considered by teachers in advance. First, is there enough space for all student projects to be included in the display? In most classrooms display space is very limited, so the answer to this initial question is probably NO.

If including every student's work is a primary objective of the display, the problem can be solved by considering **display sites outside of the classroom** itself. There are many auxiliary places within schools that can be used for displays such as corridors, lunchrooms, lobbies, gyms, staff rooms, and offices. Placing art in these areas encourages students to take pride in their school and fosters a sense of civility in parts of the school that can be difficult for teachers to supervise directly. Even if student displays can be accommodated within the school building, teachers should give some consideration to external sites such as local hospitals, nursing homes, civic centres, shopping malls, and corporation headquarters. Such settings provide excellent opportunities for raising levels of public support for art education, especially among taxpayers who do not have children in the school system.

SELECTION STRATEGIES

If not every piece of art is going to be displayed, teachers should explain the selection process to their students at the outset. Selection processes based upon student competition or teacher partiality should be scrupulously avoided. Some appropriate selection strategies include:
- asking students to display their own art on a voluntary basis
- displaying works that most clearly illustrate the learning outcomes of the lesson
- displaying art from preselected students such as:
  (a) the first 10 students on the class register
  (b) the students sitting in the desks closest to the window.

STUDENT CONSENT

Displaying every single piece of student art is not always the best course of action for teachers to take. Teachers need to be aware of the sense of **personal ownership** that students often feel towards art that they have produced. Whenever students ask that their art not be publicly displayed, their wishes should be fully respected.

There are many valid reasons why students might not wish to have their art displayed. For example:
- students may fear being **ridiculed by peers** if their art is placed alongside more proficient work
- student art can exhibit **errors** that, if displayed, could be mistakenly repeated by other students
- student work may contain **personal or controversial subject matter** that should not be shared with the general public.

In all such situations, teachers need to consult with the students involved before deciding whether to proceed with displaying the art.

In cases where art teachers sense that students might be reluctant to have their work displayed due to **low levels of self-esteem**, subtle efforts may be justifiably made to obtain consent. During my years as a secondary school teacher and as a university professor, I have repeatedly discovered how insecure students of all ages can be in this regard. In some instances, students have been simply unaware of how well they have done in a particular assignment; in more disturbing episodes, students have been unable to graciously accept personal compliments no matter how sincerely they were offered.

DISPLAY EQUITY

Teachers need to ensure that all students enjoy roughly equal opportunities to have their art displayed. For exceptionally proficient art students this may mean that not all of their projects will be displayed despite their obvious worthiness. Equity is more easily achieved when art curricula involve a wide range of artistic media and a judicious blend of individual and co-operative studio assignments. Under such curricular conditions, every student is likely to produce quality work suitable for display at one time or another and the issue of display equity takes care of itself in due course. ∎

COMPETITIONS & DISPLAYS

- Irwin, R. (Ed.). (1997). *The CSEA national policy and supporting perspectives for practice guidelines.* Boucherville, PQ: Canadian Society for Education through Art.

This document offers practical support for art teachers who wish to implement high quality art curricula at either the local or provincial level.

The following policies relate specifically to art competitions and displays:

- CSEA supports art programmes that provide opportunities for students to attend exhibitions of art outside of the classroom.

- CSEA opposes art competitions for elementary age students.

- CSEA strongly supports art exhibitions by elementary, secondary, and tertiary art students.

- CSEA supports juried art exhibitions by secondary and tertiary art students, if the jurying process provides pre-set criteria and individualized responses to participants. (p. 12)

PRACTICE

ARTISTIC DISCLOSURE

Self-disclosure refers to information that individuals are willing and able to share about themselves with other people. This process was developed in the late 1950s as a technique used in group therapy and individual psychoanalysis.

Disclosure is not the same as expression. It denotes a more deliberate approach to artistic activity that reflects process as well as product, and ability in addition to attitude.

Art gives disclosure a physical expression which can be taken apart or *deconstructed* (*see Topic 15: Postmodernism*) to reveal information about:

- ourselves
  self-disclosure
- the artist(s) who made the art
  self- or *cultural*-disclosure
- the context in which the art was made
  cultural-disclosure.

As such, it complements the academic rigors of discipline-based art curricula and the cultural emphases of postmodernism which include:

- the primacy of meaning over form
- the critical role of self in society
- the rising importance of popular art.

TOPIC 11
THE ARTIST

I have not yet directly addressed the question, *"What is art?"* Since this particular section is devoted to conceptions of the artist, it is probably a good place to clarify what I mean by the word **art**. I might begin by saying that the concept of art is not universally shared. Many First Nations in Canada and aboriginal peoples elsewhere around the globe do not have any equivalent word in their languages. Even within Western countries little consensus exists as to what art *is* although greater agreement can generally be found as to what art *is not*. The ambiguity of art does occasionally provoke public debate, but only when preceded by an expenditure of tax dollars or an exposure to nude bodies.

For educators, the ambiguity of art presents difficulties of an entirely different nature. In the present climate of administrative accountability and parental involvement, many teachers find themselves increasingly reluctant to implement parts of curricula which they consider to be inherently subjective.

This is especially true for art where curricular guidelines and teacher inservice are often nonexistent. Consequently, even fundamental questions about teaching art perplex most classroom teachers:

- Can young children produce genuine art?
- Do craft projects qualify as art activities?
- How can artistic expression be assessed?

Such questions can only be answered after a consensus has been reached about the nature of art itself.

ART AS DISCLOSURE

Most school art curricula remain philosophically **modernist**. As a result, the modernist emphasis upon originality and supremacy of form over meaning provide benchmarks for deciding what constitutes art. In such curricula, child art is suspect due to most children's inability to replicate their art and their reliance upon formulaic imagery. Similarly, crafts seldom qualify as art due to their technical simplicity and design uniformity. Matters of assessment are relegated to a small circle of professional art critics.

Personally, I believe that modernist criteria are fundamentally elitist and exclusionary. Given the advent of postmodernism in most other artistic spheres, school art must find a new conceptual foundation. I propose that **disclosure** be that foundation, and that school curricula focus on what artists and viewers reveal about self and culture through the act of producing or responding to art. Disclosure-based art is discussed more fully in the Practice window.

PLATE 1   JOHN MacGREGOR   *Interplanetary Voyage*   1967

PLATE 2   DENNIS BURTON   *Newark, New Jersey, July 11 1967 or Across the Peace Bridge*   1968

PLATE 3   kerry ferris   *sunset - metamorphosis one*   1985/86

PLATE 4   BOB ZARSKI   *Millenium*   1980

CONCEPTIONS OF THE ARTIST

Students often justify their decision not to study art after elementary school by saying, *"I'm not an artist."* When pressed to explain what they mean, many apologetically claim that, *"I can't draw a straight line"* or the classic, *"I'm just not creative."* To understand why these explanations are offered so frequently we need to do some research into historical, Western conceptions of the artist.

Kearney Model

Richard Kearney has developed a paradigmatic model which traces shifts in Western attitudes towards imagination. With a little gentle massaging I believe that his research can suit our purposes quite well. Kearney's model consists of 3 paradigms or **world views**: premodernist, modernist, and postmodernist.

The **premodernist** artist sought to replicate the divine handiwork of God, the original Creator. Physical mastery over materials such as stone, wood, and paint became the trademark of an accomplished artist, a conception of the artist which remains expressed in the assumed importance of drawing straight lines. The metaphor for this *reproductive* paradigm is a mirror reflecting transcendental light from God.

The **modernist** artist, on the other hand, strove to improve upon God's creation. Intellectual mastery over ideals such as beauty, truth, nature, space, and proportion became the new benchmarks for artistic recognition, a conception of the artist which resonates even today in the perceived need to be creative. The metaphor for this *productive* paradigm is the proverbial lamp of knowledge.

Finally, the **postmodernist** artist seeks to critique and challenge contemporary culture. An ability to construct meaning through the use of allegories, metaphors, and narrative elements assist these artists in their task. This conception of the artist has yet to find any general reflection in school art curricula. The metaphor for this *parodic* paradigm is a looking glass mirror which looks in upon itself *ad infinitum*.

While Kearney's model is based chronologically, I am not attributing any linear or progressive qualities to these Western conceptions of the artist · all are of equal legitimacy and value. What I am proposing, however, is that we look at how our art curricula are structured in light of this model. Do our studio activities nurture each of these conceptions, or just the one with which we feel most comfortable? Perhaps more students would continue with art if we helped more of them find the artist within, and ensuring that our curricula reflect each of these conceptions of the artist is a step in that direction. ■

RESEARCH

ART & ARTISTS

- Clark, R. (1987). *Aesthetic self-disclosure in visual arts*. Unpublished doctoral manuscript. University of Toronto.

- _____. (1994). *Art education: A Canadian perspective*. Toronto, ON: Ontario Society for Education through Art.

- _____. (1996). *Art education: Issues in postmodernist pedagogy*. Reston, VA: National Art Education Association.

- Feldman, E. (1982). *The artist*. Toronto, ON: Prentice Hall.

- Kearney, R. (1988). *The wake of imagination: Toward a postmodern culture*. Minneapolis, MN: University of Minnesota Press.

- Smith, A. (1993). *Getting into art history*. Toronto, ON: Barn Press.

PRACTICE

EXPERIENTIAL ACTIVITIES

What do you remember about art history classes in high school .. memorizing dates .. lights out .. or slide recognition tests? Well, Annie Smith's *Getting into Art History* is packed with really fun teaching ideas which allow students to experience styles of expression through studio such as:

- **Extend the Picture**
  Start with a landscape or portrait and have your students continue the lines, shapes, and colours beyond the borders of the original work.

- **Complete a Fragment**
  Provide your students with a small part of an unfamiliar work of art and ask them to complete a composition. Later, compare their works to the original.

- **Walk In and Turn Around**
  Using a landscape or interior work, let your students depict what they would see if they stood in the centre and looked left, right, above, or behind.

- **Neo We've Seen Everything**
  Ask your students to re-design a mail box, fire hydrant, bike rack, or telephone in an Egyptian, Classical, Gothic, or Renaissance revivalist style.

TOPIC 12
STYLES OF EXPRESSION

Young children love to express themselves through art media such as paint, paper, and plasticine. Questions of style do not interfere with their willing disclosure of ideas, whether real or imagined. This spontaneity of expression is a characteristic of child art (*see Topic 2: Art Development*) that delights parents and early childhood educators alike; in the literature it is called **creative expressionism**. Early 20th century educators such as Frank Cizek became convinced that children develop artistic skills naturally as part of overall cognitive, motor, and affective maturation. Creative expressionists contend that the spontaneity of expression found in child art is negatively affected by adult instruction, and that the widely-documented decline in adolescent art is directly attributable to repressive school curricula.

IMPEDIMENTS TO EXPRESSION

As children grow older, they become increasingly conscious of the adult world around them. By the middle of elementary school, this heightened awareness manifests itself as students become reluctant to engage in activities that they associate with childhood. Such noncompliant behaviour is actually a perfectly natural and positive sign of maturation - the students are asking to be treated as young adults. In skill- or performance-based activities, their fear of being treated like a child or teased by classmates is especially painful, and classroom teachers ignore such anxieties at their own peril. In extreme cases, students will deliberately misbehave in order to be sent out of the room, preferring the certainty of detention over the chance of humiliation.

In art, this phenomenon is referred to as **dawning realism**. As the name implies, students become fixated on realistic forms of artistic expression because they erroneously equate realism with adult art. The problem here lies in the inability of young artists to achieve an acceptable degree of proficiency in realistic studio techniques. More often than not, adolescent attempts at realistic expression prompt even greater levels of peer ridicule and personal embarrassment. For most students this frustration signals the end of their artistic development and a gradual regression to the level of child art.

This problem can be addressed by introducing students to **surrealistic**, **abstract**, and **non-objective** styles of artistic expression, forms of adult art which are not so dependent upon advanced studio skills. This simple strategy can be hampered, however, by generalist teachers' limited knowledge of art history, a dearth of age-appropriate instructional resources, inadequate time allowances for art, and limited access to courses of study prepared by provincial ministries of education or local boards of education.

PEDAGOGIC CONSIDERATIONS

Watching Your Terminology

Educators from non-art backgrounds are often perplexed by the lack of standardized terminology in art curricula. For example, while all texts stress the need to teach elements and principles of composition, the individual elements and principles listed vary widely from author to author (*see Topic 14: Formalism*). Even basic terms such as **abstract art** and **expressive art** are frequently used to convey conflicting ideas. In a general sense, all art is simultaneously abstract and expressive; even realistic art expresses just one artist's perception of the physical world. In a specific sense, however, abstract and expressive refer to stylistic contrasts which exist between works rooted in logic and works focused on emotion.

Choosing Your Approach

Once you decide to introduce your students to styles of expression you are immediately confronted with a menu of different curricular approaches. Choosing one specific model is not an easy task but a careful appraisal of your teaching situation will help you decide which option is likely the most appropriate. Traditionally, styles of expression have been organized **chronologically** and linked to historical periods; this is not a wise choice for primary teachers whose young students cannot grasp time or geography. The **monumental** approach introduces students to exemplars which illustrate various stylistic attributes. **Biographies** can also be used quite effectively to lend styles of expression a more human dimension. Finally, **thematic** and **experiential** approaches which merge studio with art history have become quite popular in recent years (*see the Practice window for more details*).

Selecting Your Exemplars

Take comfort in knowing that the selection of stylistic exemplars is a major task even for art specialists. I hope that the following points will help you put this politically sensitive process into some perspective:

- Accept that you can't teach everything that you would like your students to learn.
  This would not be possible no matter how much additional time you devoted to art.
- Try to avoid an overtly Eurocentric emphasis in your selection of stylistic exemplars.
  Include works from different cultures, continents, and centuries. Don't forget Canada, eh?
- Make a conscious effort not to compare apples with oranges.
  Compare African masks with European masks, and Gothic cathedrals with Islamic mosques.
- Be sensitive to the diversity of students in your class.
  Check to see that your exemplars were not all produced by dead, white males.

ART HISTORY

- Bennett, B., & Hall, C. (1984). *Discovering Canadian art: Learning the language.* Toronto, ON: Prentice Hall.

- Feldman, B. (1982). *The artist.* Toronto, ON: Prentice Hall.

- _____. (1987). *Varieties of visual experience* (3rd ed.). Toronto, ON: Prentice Hall.

- Fichner-Rathus, L. (1995). *Understanding art* (4th ed.). Toronto, ON: Prentice Hall.

- Fleming, W. (1991). *Arts & ideas* (8th ed.). Toronto, ON: Holt, Rinehart and Winston.

- Janson, H. (1986). *A basic history of art* (2nd ed.). Toronto, ON: Prentice Hall.

- MacGregor, R., Hall, C., Bennett, B., & Calvert, A. (1987). *Canadian art: Building a heritage.* Toronto, ON: Prentice Hall.

- Smith, A. (1993). *Getting into art history.* Toronto, ON: Barn Press.

CONSTRUCTING A STYLE CONTINUUM

STYLE AS AN EXPRESSION OF REALITY

Art has traditionally been linked to historical eras such as the Renaissance, a practice which has favoured chronologically-based art history texts like *A Basic History of Art* (Janson, 1986). In recent years it has become clear, though, that this approach presents Eurocentric art as a universal standard against which all other art can, perhaps even should, be measured.

Many art historians, therefore, are turning to biographical, experiential, and thematic formats which more readily accommodate non-Western styles of artistic expression. Given the educational focus of this book and the need for teachers to meet the challenges posed by adolescent fixations with realism, I have constructed a continuum which thematically organizes artistic styles as expressions of reality.

Artists in all cultures have had to decide whether or not the physical world offered an appropriate context for expressing their thoughts and emotions. Although in our Western culture physical reality has long been considered the expressive ideal, imaginary worlds replete with dragons and vengeful gods have also provided artists with alternative expressions of reality. Similarly, artists who have distorted or simply ignored the physical world have lived all over the globe, not just in New York lofts or Paris cafés.

Thus, it is important to understand that the four points along this style continuum · **surrealistic**, **realistic**, **abstract**, and **non-objective** · were not chosen because of their compatibility with historical eras in Western art but their ability to incorporate non-Western artistic expressions of reality. Due to the introductory nature of this book, however, and the nationalistic mandates of Canadian art curricula, Western exemplars will be featured.

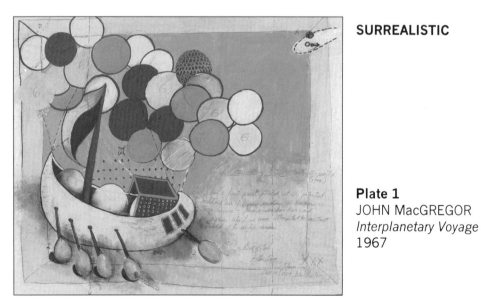

SURREALISTIC

Plate 1
JOHN MacGREGOR
Interplanetary Voyage
1967

REALISTIC

Plate 2
DENNIS BURTON
*Newark, New Jersey,
July 11 1967 or
Across the Peace Bridge*
1968

CONTINUUM

USING THE CONTINUUM

As is often the case with organizational typologies, locating complex and interrelated elements along a continuum is never a neat and tidy process. Even though by its very definition a continuum implies a structural fluidity and an absence of discrete categories, there is always a tendency to lose sight of the **numerous gradations** which fall between points along the line.

This is especially true for multi-faceted constructs like artistic expression, where individual works can simultaneously contain multiple characteristics which defy singular categorization. Compounding this phenomenon is the factor of **time**. With some notable exceptions, such as ancient Egyptian art which remained essentially static for thousands of years, the lives of artists and the history of artistic styles typically span periods of major transition.

Each of the following pages highlights one of the 4 styles in our continuum by providing a Western **historical overview** and some **stylistic exemplars**. When selecting the exemplars I tried to include well-known works which art teachers might access with relative ease in school or professional libraries. Nonetheless, I remained very conscious of the futility of listing exemplars in a book without providing any corresponding reproductions. As a form of partial compensation, I restricted my selections to those found in two standard art history texts and included a page reference for each exemplar:

- for **international exemplars** see *Arts & Ideas* (8 th ed.) (Fleming, 1991)
- for **Canadian exemplars** see *Canadian Art: Building a Heritage* (MacGregor, Hall, Bennett, & Calvert, 1987) *page references for Canadian works are indicated by* **bold** *type* ■

ABSTRACT

Plate 3
kerry ferris
sunset - metamorphosis one
1985/86

NON-OBJECTIVE

Plate 4
BOB ZARSKI
Millenium
1980

CONTINUUM

SURREALISTIC

Religion has played an important role in the artistic expression of cultures throughout history. Certainly, this has been true of Western art from pagan fertility amulets to Christian frescoes in the Vatican. This interplay between art and religion has resulted in some of the most astonishing imagery ever created, for artists have had to reach beyond the physical world for their representations of good and evil.

Fantasy, therefore, represents an age-old expression of reality that in the 20th century has been labeled surrealistic. The Bible, along with the Torah and the Koran, provides fantastic descriptions of heaven and hell which artists such as Hieronymus Bosch and Gislebertus expressed in their works *Garden of Earthly Delights* and *Last Judgement*. In an era of cheap horror movies and gimmicky special effects, it is difficult for us to fully appreciate how literally their frightening images were interpreted by Medieval viewers.

Dadaism was a form of anti-art which appeared briefly at the end of the First World War; *dada* is a child's word in French referring to a hobbyhorse. Dadaists produced bitterly satirical art and political manifestos which set the stage for later surrealistic expressions of reality in the 1930s and 40s.

Psychic automatism is not a very widely known style today because it has been subsumed within the more ubiquitous term surrealism. Essentially, psychic automatists sought to express psychological realities like dreams, phobias, and complexes directly · bypassing reason entirely. While works such as Salvador Dali's *The Persistence of Memory* are somewhat disturbing other surrealistic works by Paul Klee and Joan Miró are quite uplifting.

The moody uncertainty of *The Persistence of Memory* typifies the general sense of unease generated in a more recent form of surrealistic expression known as **magic realism**. As the name implies, such works appear at first glance to be quite conventional but, upon closer inspection, the presence of paranormal activity is suggested, which leaves the viewer uncertain as to what the artist's real message might have been. ∎

SURREALISTIC EXPRESSIONS OF REALITY IN WESTERN ART

Fantasy
HIERONYMUS BOSCH. *Garden of Earthly Delights.* c. 1500. 293
SANDRO BOTTICELLI. *Birth of Venus.* c. 1480. 254
MARC CHAGALL. *I and the Village.* 1911. 540
GEORGIO de CHIRICO. *The Menacing Muses.* 1917. 560
GISLEBERTUS. *Last Judgement.* c. 1130-35. 159
FRANCISCO GOYA. *Saturn Devouring One of His Children.* 1820-23. 465
EL GRECO. *Burial of Count Orgaz.* 1586. 359
TERRY SHOFFNER. *Train on Zipper.* 1981. **88**

Dadaism & Anti-Art
MARCEL DUCHAMP. *L.H.O.O.Q.* 1919. 540

Psychic Automatism
SALVADOR DALI. *The Persistence of Memory.* 1931. 541
PAUL KLEE. *Around the Fish.* 1926. 542
JOAN MIRÓ. *Personages with Star.* 1933. 543

Magic Realism
DEREK MICHAEL BESANT. *Flatiron Mural.* 1980. **89**
ALEX COLVILLE. *Western Star.* 1985. **38**

REALISTIC

Artists in Western societies have traditionally sought to replicate the physical world in their paintings and sculptures. Art that appears to contemporary viewers as abstract, naive, or neo-primitive should be carefully scrutinized for original expressive intent; such works often turn out to be examples of realistic expression, albeit not very convincing ones.

Classical Greek art was famous for its realistic statues of the human body but other critically important conventions for replicating the real world, such as linear perspective, remained undiscovered until the Renaissance. Roman artists copied Greek paintings and cast replicas of Greek statues.

During the **Medieval** period, realism found validation in Biblical claims that God created the universe and that mankind was created in His image. As a result of the chaos created by the demise of the Roman Empire, however, Classical techniques for realistic expression were essentially lost.

Renewed interest and research into Classical art during the **Renaissance**, along with concurrent discoveries in science and mathematics, allowed artists to master realistic expression. Realism continued to dominate Western art during the **Baroque**, **Neo-classical**, and **Romantic** eras.

Western art's long fascination with realistic expression was profoundly affected by the widespread introduction of photography in the mid-1800s. Almost overnight, replicating the physical world in paint or stone seemed pointless and strangely uncreative. For the next hundred years realistic expression remained unfashionable, while a seemingly endless stream of abstract, non-objective, and surrealistic styles of *avant-garde* modernist art dominated the walls of art galleries and the attention of art critics.

A resurgence of artistic interest in realistic expression was inevitable, and by the mid-1970s **new realism** had achieved a level of popular interest and critical respectability. Postmodernism's preference for meaning over form and its appreciation of historical styles made it acceptable once again for artists to locate personal expression in the physical world. ■

REALISTIC EXPRESSIONS OF REALITY IN WESTERN ART

Classical
Hercules Finding His Infant Son Telephus. c. A.D. 70.   70
Portrait of a Roman Lady. c. A.D. 90   95

Medieval
GIOTTO. *Joachim Returning to the Sheepfold.* 1305-06.   230
LIMBOURG BROTHERS. Duke of Berry's *Book of Hours.* c. 1415.   212

Renaissance
LEONARDO da VINCI. *Madonna of the Rocks.* c. 1483.   255
MICHELANGELO. *David.* 1501-04.   260

Baroque
JUDITH LEYSTER. *Self-Portrait.* c. 1635.   369
PETER PAUL RUBENS. *Garden of Love.* c. 1632-34.   396

Neo-Classical
JACQUES-LOUIS DAVID. *Oath of the Horatii.* 1784.   447
EUGÈNE DELACROIX. *Liberty Leading the People.* 1830.   461

Romantic
PAUL KANE. *Blackfoot Chief and Subordinates.* c. 1851-56.   **48**
CORNELIUS KRIEGHOFF. *The Horse Trader.* 1871.   **47**
LUCIUS O'BRIEN. *Sunrise on the Saguenay.* 1880.   **46**

New Realism
DIANA DABINETT. *Salmon Dinner Party.* 1981.   **86**
RICHARD ESTES. *Downtown.* 1978.   565
JOE FAFARD. *A Merchant of Pense.* 1973.   **76**
DUANE HANSON. *Supermarket Shopper.* 1970.   603
PHILIP PEARLSTEIN. *Female Model on Platform Rocker.* 1978.   601
MARY PRATT. *Split Grilse.* 1979.   **85**

ABSTRACT

The advent of photography brought to an end the historical dominance of realistic expression in Western art. Technological developments in the field of optics, however, also provided art with a whole range of exciting new styles of expression. As in the Renaissance, this marriage of art and science gave birth to an epoch noted for invention and creativity.

Impressionists were fascinated by light and painted outdoors to capture its ephemeral effects upon colour. *Impression - Sunrise* by Claude Monet provided this new movement with its name and demonstrated how daubs of colour, blended in the eye rather than on a palette, could imply shape.

From this point of departure, **postimpressionists** developed a dazzling array of new abstract styles. Georges Seurat's **pointillism** used thousands of coloured dots to achieve a greater degree of shape definition. Works by Paul Gauguin and Paul Cézanne also moved away from the fuzzy shapes so typical of impressionism by using contour lines and solid, block colours. The almost architectural construction of such paintings made the vibrancy of Vincent Van Gogh's deeply spiritual *Starry Night* all the more captivating. In Canada, Tom Thomson and the Group of Seven used postimpressionistic techniques to express the ruggedness of untouched northern landscapes.

Cubism can be traced to Pablo Picasso's *Les Demoiselles d'Avignon* with its use of multiple planes and African-inspired, geometric shapes and colours.

Whereas logic played a key role in postimpressionism, emotion took centre stage in **expressionism**. Using works by Van Gogh and Gauguin as stylistic bases, expressionists pushed their brilliant colours, exaggerated shapes, and non-realistic compositions to the very frontier of non-objective art.

Although these abstract forms of artistic expression occurred in an age of unparalleled human achievement, they also developed amidst the social devastation caused by two world wars and a global economic depression. **Social realists** tried to capture the pathos of these catastrophic events in politically motivated works such as Pablo Picasso's seminal *Guernica*. ∎

ABSTRACT EXPRESSIONS OF REALITY IN WESTERN ART

Impressionism
ÉDOUARD MANET. *Bar at the Folies-Bergère.* 1881-82. 504
CLAUDE MONET. *Japanese Bridge at Giverny.* 1900. 507
PIERRE AUGUSTE RENOIR. *La Moulin de la Galette à Montmarte.* 1876. 505

Postimpressionism
MARY CASSATT. *Boating Party.* 1893-94. 509
PAUL CÉZANNE. *Mont Ste. Victoire.* 1904-06. 513
MAURICE CULLEN. *Lévis from Québec.* 1906. **51**
PAUL GAUGUIN. *Mahana No Atua.* 1894. 511
J.E.H. MacDONALD. *Falls, Montréal River.* 1920. **55**
GEORGES SEURAT. *Sunday Afternoon on the Island of la Grande Jatte.* 1884-86. 508
TOM THOMSON. *The West Wind.* 1917. **58**
HENRI de TOULOUSE-LAUTREC. *At the Moulin Rouge.* 1892. 519
VINCENT VAN GOGH. *Starry Night.* 1889. 510

Cubism
GEORGES BRAQUE. *Oval Still Life.* 1914. 534
PABLO PICASSO. *Les Demoiselles d'Avignon.* 1907. 523

Expressionism
EMILY CARR. *Study in Movement.* 1936. **54**
LAWREN S. HARRIS. *Lake and Mountains.* 1927-28. **57**
WASSILY KANDINSKY. *Improvisation No. 30.* 1913. 533
FRANZ MARC. *The Great Blue Horses.* 1911. 533
HENRI MATISSE. *Blue Window.* 1911. 531
AMEDEO MODIGLIANI. *Yellow Sweater.* 1919. 527
EMILE NOLDE. *Dancing around the Golden Calf.* 1910. 532

Social Realism
JOSÉ CLEMENTE OROZCO. *Gods of the Modern World.* 1934. 547
PABLO PICASSO. *Guernica.* 1937. 549

NON-OBJECTIVE

No realistic imagery is employed in non-objective artistic expression. Compositions are not arranged using plants, animals, or people but elements of design such as line, shape, colour, value, and texture. While pop and conceptual art do often rely on figurative shapes, they are included for their compositional value not their representational meaning. Since such art defies objective analysis, response is inherently subjective.

The origins of non-objective art are generally attributed to expressionist Wassily Kandinsky who believed that art should replicate inner emotions. His working sketches (*improvisations*) and extended works (*compositions*) vividly showed his deep despair over prevailing social conditions in Europe.

In stark contrast, Piet Mondrian sought a new, international form of art which would be completely devoid of emotional associations. Using only rectangles and primary colours, **constructivism** maximized compositional stability but offered little opportunity for expressive variation.

Abstract expressionism, or *action painting*, attempted to make creative energy visible and concrete. Paint was poured onto large canvases in a controlled, kinesthetic process to produce a cacophony of line and colour. A less frenetic treatment was adopted by Mark Rothko, who concentrated on the saturation, or intensity, of **colour fields** within rectangular blocks.

Serialism tried to free art from the formatting confines imposed by single, rectangular frames. Variations in size, shape, colour, *et cetera* were used within similar works, and displayed as a series in the same room.

Minimalism was best exemplified in prefabricated sculptures which were designed for architectural and outdoor settings. **Conceptual art** was also found outside galleries, although without the permanency of minimalism. It was often performance-based and dismantled soon after completion.

Unlike its stylistic cousin dadaism, **pop art** enjoyed a creative compatibility with popular culture. Contemporary images and media were manipulated to produce art that spoke to the lived experiences of modern society. ∎

NON-OBJECTIVE EXPRESSIONS OF REALITY IN WESTERN ART

Constructivism
PIET MONDRIAN. *New York City 1.* 1942. 551

Abstract Expressionism
JACKSON POLLOCK. *Lucifer.* 1947. 569
JEAN-PAUL RIOPELLE. *Untitled.* 1952. **72**

Colour Field Painting
HELEN FRANKENTHALER. *Formation.* 1963. 575
BARNETT NEWMAN. *Vir Heroicus Sublimis.* 1950-51. 573
MARK ROTHKO. *Green and Maroon.* 1953. 572

Serialism
JOSEF ALBERS. *Homage to the Square.* 1964. 577
YVES GAUCHER. *Bleu, Rouge, Ochre, Jaune, Vert, Orange.* 1974. **73**
FRANK STELLA. *Singerli Variation IV.* 1968. 578

Minimalism
ISAMU NOGUCHI. *Cube.* 1968. 579
ROY LEADBEATER. *Untitled.* 1982. **37**
ROBERT MURRAY. *Swing.* 1973. **33**

Pop Art
IAIN BAXTER. *Bagged Landscape.* 1966. **74**
ROBERT RAUSCHENBERG. *Monogram.* 1955-59. 580
ANDY WARHOL. *Green Coca-Cola Bottles.* 1962. 582

Conceptual Art
CHRISTO. *Surrounded Islands.* 1983. 585

PRACTICE

INTRODUCING EXEMPLARS

In what grade should children be asked to start analyzing and discussing exemplars? Well, how about kindergarten?

Actually, teachers will encounter very little reticence to talk about art during primary grades because young children are seldom self-conscious about interacting with their classmates. The confidence thus gained during such early encounters with art can help reduce personal anxiety attacks in junior and intermediate grades.

- **Begin with Student Art**
  Don't ask young children to talk about the Sistine Chapel. Let them practise their analytic skills using art that they have made themselves and for which they have experiential understanding.

- **Model Proper Art Vocabulary**
  Use words like line, colour, balance, and contrast when talking to children about their art.

- **Access Art in the Community**
  You don't need slides or posters to introduce children to works of art. Just take a walk around your local neighbourhood. You will be amazed to see how much great art goes unnoticed.

TOPIC 13
LOOKING AT ART

Art curricula have long been excessively centred on studio production, that is to say, making art. In elementary schools this imbalance has often been referred to as the **make and take syndrome**. When our students become adults, their main contacts with art will be as consumers and patrons rather than as producers, so I suggest that teachers set aside about 1/3 of their art courses for activities which will provide the new millenium with more fully-informed consumers and culturally-aware patrons.

ART CRITICISM

Looking at art involves responding on a critical level to questions such as, *"Why do I like this work of art?"* To help students understand their **artistic preferences**, teachers need to provide instructional activities which invite students to observe, discriminate, compare, and contrast various works of art.

Art criticism often takes the form of written statements and oral discussions that describe, analyze, interpret, and judge various forms of artistic expression. Edmund Burke Feldman has developed a basic model which expands upon these four critical processes as depicted below in table 13.1. Notice that the Feldman approach moves sequentially from objective to subjective and from simple to complex in order to provide a successful, and defensible, transition from initial impression to developed opinion.

Description	What do I see?	**13.1**
Analysis	How is this work composed?	ART CRITICISM
Interpretation	What was the artist trying to say?	Feldman Model
Judgement	What do I think of this work?	

Postmodernist scholars have suggested that the Feldman approach places too much importance upon the formal qualities of art objects (*see Topic 14: Formalism*) and the subject matter originally intended by the artist. They have called for models which focus greater attention upon the meaning of art objects and the interpretation of subject matter by the viewer. Such postmodernist concerns can be addressed at least partially by using the Feldman model in reverse order and working from subjective to objective.

AESTHETICS

Looking at art also involves responding on an aesthetic level. Aesthetics is a branch of philosophy that addresses important questions such as, *"Why is this drawing considered to be a work of art?"* Aesthetics is concerned with questions of **artistic value**, as morality is concerned with questions of ethical value.

Aesthetics as Experience
One way to engage our aesthetic sense is by directly participating in the production of art. Practising artists frequently judge the value of their work by reflecting on themes of aesthetic honesty and integrity. Through the careful observation of student behaviours during studio, teachers can sense whether their students are producing art. Are the students absorbed in their work? Do they know when it is finished? Do they want to talk about their completed work? If the answer to these questions is YES, it is likely that the students have been engaged in authentic aesthetic experiences and have produced real works of art.

Aesthetics as Response
A more frequent way of engaging our aesthetic sense is by responding to art produced by others. One of the unfortunate legacies of modernism is the belief that only art critics can adequately respond to art. Elliot Eisner has developed the **theory of selective response** which shows how easy this process can be. Beginning with the proposition that what we know determines how we respond, Eisner has proposed six **frames of reference** which everybody can use when they look at art: experiential, formal, symbolic, thematic, material, and contextual. Collectively, these 6 frames of reference constitute a postmodernist approach to art (*see Topic 15: Postmodernism*) which places greater importance on meaning over form, and the interpretation of meaning by viewers over the intended meaning of the artist. ∎

ART APPRECIATION

- Barrett, T. (1994). *Criticizing art: Understanding the contemporary.* Mountain View, CA: Mayfield.

- Feldman, E. (1987). *Varieties of visual experience* (3rd ed.). Toronto, ON: Prentice Hall.

- Lanier, V. (1982). *The arts we see.* New York, NY: Teachers College Press.

- Ontario Ministry of Education. (1990). *Viewing art: Intermediate and senior divisions.* Toronto, ON: Author.

- Perkins, D. (1994). *The intelligent eye: Learning to think by looking at art.* Los Angeles, CA: Getty Center for Education in the Arts.

- Smith A. (1993). *Getting into art history.* Toronto, ON: Barn Press.

Experiential	how the work affects the viewer
Formal	how the work is composed
Symbolic	how the symbols used affect the meaning of the work
Thematic	how the subject matter affects the viewer's response
Material	how the materials used affect the meaning of the work
Contextual	how the cultural milieu affected the production of the work

13.2
AESTHETICS
Eisner Model

PRACTICE

INTUITION, LOGIC, & ART

When I was a student in elementary school I recall many times being asked to create *a pleasing composition* in art assignments. This concept was never really explained by any of my teachers, but since I usually got an *A* in art I just assumed that my designs must have met the criteria for *pleasing*.

Today as an art teacher, however, I can look back and see how unfair such vague instructions must have been to the other students who needed more instructional guidance. Formalism, with its emphasis on elements & principles of composition, is often cast in a negative light by adults who are able to create art intuitively; for them, formalism is formulaic and a block to creativity. What they fail to realize is that left-brain thinkers find the logical structure of formalism a way to make sense out of an otherwise mysterious act. I believe that teachers need to value both logical and intuitive approaches to artistic expression so that a greater percentage of students find personal success in art.

The notion that creative work is always unplanned and emergent is a modernist myth that has done art education a great disservice. Give formalism an honest try - you might be *pleasantly* surprised!

TOPIC 14
FORMALISM

Art is a visual language that allows individuals to communicate their ideas with a degree of physical and aesthetic precision. Formalism refers to the **vocabulary and syntax** of this visual language. In recent years, postmodernist scholars have criticized formalism for what they perceive as its:

- undue emphasis upon the compositional content of art
- lack of attention to the cultural context in which art is made.

So, to facilitate a better balance between artistic form and meaning, I suggest that **contextual research** into **subject matter**, **biographical information**, and **stylistic influences** precede compositional analysis.

ELEMENTS & PRINCIPLES OF COMPOSITION

The **elements** of composition are generally considered to involve **line**, **shape**, **colour**, **value**, and **texture**. Compositional elements are the vocabulary which artists use to give their ideas physical expression. Not all of the elements are used in every work of art; for example, the sculpture in figure 14.1 lacks colour. Nor are the elements given equal emphasis within works of art; artists customarily compose works of art so that one or two of the elements are in a position of visual dominance over the others. The **principles** of composition typically consist of **unity**, **balance**, **contrast**, **emphasis**, and **movement**. Compositional principles result from a syntactic arrangement of one or more of the basic elements, therefore, principles must be explicitly related back to the elements. For instance, in figure 14.1 the principle of contrast has been achieved through contrasting values, that is, with highlights and shadows.

SUBJECTIVITY

While many aspects of formalism are objective by nature, such as the lack of colour in *Genesis Revisited*, teachers must accept subjective student responses, provided that adequate explanations are offered. There are many reasons why formalist analyses may differ from one person to another. Some reasons are simply physical. For example, the visual importance of elements or principles of composition can change when viewers step forward to inspect details more closely. Other reasons are aesthetic and relate to Elliot Eisner's six **frames of reference** that viewers employ when contemplating works of art: experiential, formal, symbolic, thematic, material, and contextual (*see Topic 13: Looking at Art*). The subjectivity of formalism should be considered as a curricular strength, for it helps students learn to cope with ambiguity and experience nuance - two of the primary reasons why art is taught in schools.

14.1
ROGER CLARK
Genesis Revisited 1982
Plaster and vermiculite
66 x 46 cm.
Collection of the artist

ROGER CLARK
b. 1953 Brantford, Ontario, Canada

Roger Clark studied architecture before he entered the teaching profession in 1976. This architectural influence can be seen in the graphic quality of his figure drawing *Seated Nude Wearing Boots*, shown on page 25, and his sculpture *Genesis Revisited*.

STYLISTIC INFLUENCES

Genesis Revisited is a typical example of **abstract expression** of reality. Stylistically it can be considered **cubist** (*see page 48*).

An offshoot of cubist art, **futurism** was founded in 1910. Futurists were excited by the beauty of industrial imagery such as *the machine*. The visual vocabulary of futurism was defined by Italian sculptors Umberto Boccioni and Giacomo Balla who attempted to represent movement within their art. The many mechanical forms in *Genesis Revisited* are typically futuristic, and the concentric shapes around the main focal point are reminiscent of the glowing shapes around the lamp in Balla's *Streetlight* (1913).

SUBJECT MATTER

Genesis Revisited depicts the Biblical story of creation as given in the Book of Genesis. The hand of God appears in the upper left corner as a heavily abstracted, mechanical shape; it provides a sharp contrast to the gentle hand of God depicted by Michelangelo in *The Creation of Adam* (1508-12). There are several other abstracted shapes in *Genesis Revisited* such as the sun and moon in the upper right, some plants in the lower left, and a bird in the lower right corner.

This **relief** sculpture consists of 2 panels; the upper represents heaven, the lower represents the Earth. Works of art that consist of 2 pieces, whether two- or three-dimensional, are called **diptychs**. ■

FORMALIST ANALYSIS

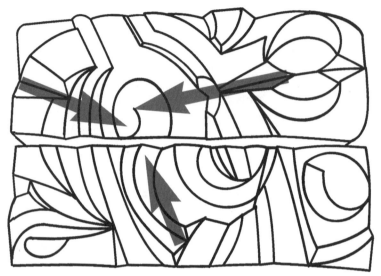

14.2
LINE

14.3
SHAPE

ELEMENTS OF COMPOSITION

Line

Strictly speaking, no lines have been used in this compositional design. Nonetheless, I think that most viewers will have a general feeling that several implicit, directional lines extend radially from the abstracted hand which provides the main focal point for this work (*see diagram 14.2: Line*).

Shape

As is the case with almost all sculptural art, *Genesis Revisited* relies heavily upon the element of shape. In particular, there are 4 deeply abstracted shapes which help establish the original narrative intended by the artist. In the upper panel, which represents heaven, the shape on the left side is the hand of God reaching down to create Earth; the shapes on the right are the sun and moon. In the lower panel, which represents the Earth, there are abstracted plant shapes on the left and an abstracted bird on the right.

Colour

No colours have been used in this composition; neutrals such as black, white, grey, and brown are considered to be non-colours in art.

Value

The most important element in this work is value (*see 14.1 on page 53*). Sculptural compositions can change very dramatically when light sources change direction. Not only can the mood be altered from joy to sadness, but changes in light direction can cause surface features to advance or retreat, depending upon the degree to which they are either highlighted or shadowed. Focal points are especially vulnerable to changes in value. When analyzing three-dimensional works of art, it is always a good idea to make a note of the lighting conditions under which the analysis was made.

Texture

If you run your fingers over the surface of this sculpture, you will find that the texture of the plaster is remarkably smooth. If you consider the entire top surface as a textural plane, however, the relief itself is very coarse. ■

14.4
BALANCE

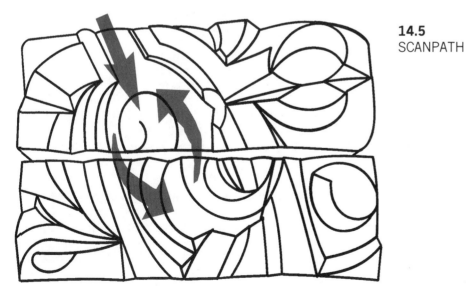

14.5
SCANPATH

PRINCIPLES OF COMPOSITION

Unity
Compositional unity has been achieved in *Genesis Revisited* through a radial pattern which has as its central hub the space inside the abstracted hand. The compositional importance of this main focal point complements the key role played by God in the narrative of creation in the Book of Genesis.

Balance
The numerous shapes in this sculpture radiate from the main focal point which was balanced asymmetrically about the vertical axis (1/3 to the left and 2/3 to the right) and symmetrically (50/50) about the horizontal axis (*see diagram 14.4: Balance*).

Contrast
The principle of contrast has been applied mainly to the element of value. The heavily delineated shapes produce very strong highlights and shadows causing each of the shapes to advance or recede from the sculptural plane. Without such contrasting values, the myriad of shapes in *Genesis Revisited* would lose their compositional harmony and appear as nothing more than a jumble of competing lines (*see diagram 14.3: Shape*).

Emphasis
Whenever works of art are designed around a single, major focal point it is important that the various elements of composition work in unison to support that emphasis. Although *Genesis Revisited* contains many diverse, abstracted shapes and dramatic changes in value, they are distributed evenly about the focal point. The net effect is an overall consistency of visual interest which maintains the importance of the major focal point.

Movement
Regardless of where the viewer's attention is initially captured, the radial composition moves the viewer's visual scanpath into the central hub. Subsequently, the concentric shapes which surround the focal point help ensure that the entire work is scanned (*see diagram 14.5: Scanpath*). ■

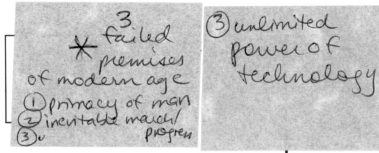

TOPIC 15
POSTMODERNISM

POSTMODERNISM & DBAE

Since the early 1980s, the acceptance of discipline-based art education (DBAE) has steadily increased across North America in secondary and post-secondary schools. Coincidentally, postmodernist influences have also made inroads in art curricula at the secondary and post-secondary levels. Many art specialists remain divided as to whether or not these two curricular forces are compatible.

This book is premised on my personal belief that DBAE can, indeed, meet the challenges posed by postmodernism by:

- introducing non-traditional media and technologies
- exploring non-Western concepts of space and design
- expanding established artistic canons to include non-Western exemplars
- exposing students to art produced by hiddenstream artists.

I have tried to illustrate how these 4 basic principles can enrich traditional forms of art instruction in the **Images of Women** unit found on pages 58 & 59. Although I have labeled this unit *reconstructive* due to its reconstructive sequence, my personal response to postmodernism is probably more accurately described as reformist.

On a cold, moonless night in April 1912, *RMS Titanic* collided with an iceberg and started to sink. Our enduring fascination with the *Titanic* cannot be explained by the loss of 1,500 lives on that fateful voyage, for the 20th century has given us more appalling stories of death and destruction. The *Titanic* lingers in our collective, cultural psyche not as a maritime calamity but a sobering reminder of the failed premises of the modern age: the innate primacy of man, the inevitable march of progress, and the unlimited power of technology. Since all three of these modernist constructs found their physical expression in the *Titanic*, the loss of the *unsinkable* ocean liner pales in comparison to the loss of the grand ideals which it represented. The notion of *truth* was the *Titanic*'s most significant casualty.

CONCEPTS IN POSTMODERNISM

Unlike modernism, postmodernism is not an artistic style but rather a cultural phenomenon which has resulted from an **erosion of public confidence in humanist ideals** such as logic, progress, and science. For individuals accustomed to the buoyant optimism of modernism, the sense of doubt which pervades postmodernism causes deep consternation. Where advocates of postmodernism see noble intent and liberating action, proponents of modernism tend to see only nihilistic attitude and destructive critique.

Although postmodernism is routinely expressed differently in specific disciplines, there are three basic concepts common to all postmodernist theories: poststructuralism, deconstruction, and reconstruction.

Poststructuralism
Poststructuralism contends that knowledge is socially constructed by ordinary, fallible human beings. Correspondingly, there are no divinely-inspired or universal forms of knowledge, only *grand narratives* like history and science which offer subjective interpretations of reality that tend to relegate those objectified to positions of inferiority. This subject/object dynamic formed the core of many modernist theories such as feminism (*male/female*), Marxism (*capitalist/socialist*), and political science (*conservative/liberal*).

Deconstruction/Reconstruction
Logically speaking, whatever has been socially *constructed* by individuals or groups of people can be taken apart to expose the social forces embedded within; in the literature, this called *deconstruction*. The personal perspectives, or *world views*, which drive the deconstructive process produce a predictable diversity of *reconstructed* interpretations in a phenomenon generally referred to as reconstruction.

POSTMODERNISM & ART

The purposeful uncertainty which characterizes postmodernist theory has greatly affected art, as well. Whereas modernist art emphasized the **purity of universal forms** such as line, shape, colour, and value, postmodernist art is concerned with multiple **interpretations of cultural meaning**. In most instances, postmodernist art speaks to the complexity of our contemporary existence through paradoxes and visual contradictions which result from the deliberate interplay of incongruent artistic styles and media.

The Postmodernist Artist
Thanks largely to research undertaken by feminists, the modernist myth of a male, heroic genius making solitary leaps into previously unknown realms of creative expression has been shown to be fraudulent. Today, we have a much greater understanding of the cultural dynamics which spawn great works of art.

The Postmodernist Viewer
The modernist preference for fine art and deference to an *avant-garde* core of art critics has been replaced by the postmodernist predilection for popular culture and dependence upon corporate tastes. As a result, the interpretation of art is no longer the prerogative of artists or critics but the right of individuals or groups, regardless of whether they are part of the mainstream or *hiddenstream* culture.

The Postmodernist Market
The creation of art is increasingly seen as a collective activity involving educators, critics, historians, entrepreneurs, and consumers. Recent advances in mass communication and reproductive technologies have promoted a greater commodification of art and participation by previously marginalized groups.

CURRICULAR RESPONSES TO POSTMODERNISM

Broadly speaking, curricular responses to postmodernist theory fall into one or other of 2 categories: **reformist** or **reconstructionist**. Reformists believe that traditional art curricula, such as discipline-based art education (DBAE), can be readily adapted to accommodate the most important issues raised by postmodernism (*see the Practice window for more information on reformist approaches and DBAE*). On the other hand, reconstructionists contend that most traditional art curricula are implacably at odds with postmodernism and need to be replaced. A reconstructive unit is modeled on pages 58 & 59. ■

POSTMODERNISM & ART

- Clark, R. (1996). *Art education: Issues in postmodernist pedagogy.* Reston, VA: National Art Education Association.

- Efland, A., Freedman, K., & Stuhr, P. (Eds.). *Postmodern art education: An approach to curriculum.* Reston, VA: National Art Education Association.

- Giroux, H. (1992). *Border crossings: Cultural workers and the politics of education.* New York, NY: Routledge.

- Kearney, R. (1988). *The wake of imagination: Toward a postmodern culture.* Minneapolis, MN: University of Minnesota Press.

- Lyotard, J. (1984). *The postmodern condition: A report on knowledge.* Minneapolis, MN: University of Minnesota Press. (Trans. by G. Bennington & B. Massumi).

- Yakel, N. (Ed.). (1992). *The future: Challenge of change.* Reston, VA: National Art Education Association.

A RECONSTRUCTIVE UNIT

RECONSTRUCTIVE RESPONSES TO POSTMODERNISM

Conceptions of Culture
Reconstructionists believe that traditional art curricula are incapable of adequately responding to the challenges posed by postmodernist theory. They make this claim based on the innate differences which exist between anthropology/sociology/ethnography and social criticism in regard to **culture**. Whereas the former disciplinary trio conceptualizes culture as a way of life wherein human beings all work together to support the whole, social criticism envisages culture as a way of conflict wherein groups with competing interests exist in a state of constant social tension.

The Nature of Reconstructive Curricula
Reconstructive curricula differ from traditional curricula in 3 main areas:

- *Traditional Curricula*
  cultural functionalism
  social individualism
  cautious reform
- *Reconstructive Curricula*
  cultural conflict
  social collectivism
  radical reconstruction.

Planning Reconstructive Curricula
Reconstructive curricula are intended to foster a sense of cultural relativity and cultural perspective among all students, whether they be members of the dominant cultural group or some significantly marginalized minority.

Typically, reconstructive curricula reflect the following planning sequence:
- units begin by tapping into the lived experiences of students
- lived experiences are given a wider, historical perspective
- appropriate cross-cultural comparisons are undertaken
- alternative futures and scenarios for change are articulated.

This planning sequence can be seen in the accompanying reconstructive unit **Images of Women** which was designed for senior level art students.

STAGE 1: Lived Experiences

IMAGES OF WOMEN IN WESTERN CULTURE

ACTIVITY 1

Culture & Group Identity
The students will explore images of women from their own community including family members, neighbours, and friends. This first assignment should demonstrate the diversity of visual images used to depict women.

Assignment
- *Produce a 5-minute slide presentation with an accompanying sound track which documents the diversity of images of women in the local community.*
  or
- *Create a photo montage with accompanying didactic panels which documents the diversity of images of women in the local community.*

ACTIVITY 2

Culture & Personal Identity
In this second assignment the students will examine how images of women can convey individuality by comparing these two specific Canadian works:
Plate 2: *Newark, New Jersey, July 11 1967* or *Across the Peace Bridge*
Plate 3: *sunset - metamorphosis one* (represents ferris and her son).

Assignment
- *Write a 750 word paper comparing the images of women in these 2 works.*
- *Select an image from Lesson 1 which closely parallels either Plate 2 or 3. Paint that image using the same stylistic techniques used by Burton or ferris.*

STAGE 2: Cross-Cultural Comparisons

IMAGES OF WOMEN IN NON-WESTERN CULTURES

ACTIVITY 3

Culture & Religion
In this lesson the students will conduct computer searches to discover how women have been visually depicted in the religious art of a wide variety of faith communities. The students will be encouraged to work in small groups with classmates who are researching different religious affiliations.

Assignment
- *Use either dust or oil pastels to depict a female religious character from your research. Use a word processing programme to prepare appropriate didactic information about this particular woman.*

ACTIVITY 4

Culture & Family
Each student will be randomly assigned a country from Asia or Africa to study for patterns of family life. Special attention will be focused on the role(s) played by Asian or African women in their domestic relationships.

Assignment
- *Genre works by Western artists which depict women in domestic situations will be catalogued by theme and assembled into an art history data file.*
- *A similar file will be assembled from genre works by Asian or African artists.*
- *Using media of their own choice, the students will illustrate a specific aspect of contemporary family life in their assigned country.*

STAGE 3: Alternative Futures

IMAGES OF WOMEN IN THE NEW MILLENIUM

ACTIVITY 5

Culture & Change
Cultures are never static since they are continually responding to change. In this assignment the students will identify a specific aspect of modern life that impacts negatively upon women. Subsequently, student groups will brainstorm how that aspect can be eliminated in the new millenium.

Assignment
- *Working in groups of 4 or 5 the students will illustrate how life will be better for women in the new millenium in regard to the identified problem area. Each group will construct either a 3-D diorama or a mixed media mural.*

ACTIVITY 6

Culture & Tradition
Paradoxically, the other constant element of culture is the maintenance of tradition. In this final lesson, the students will identify what single image of women they would most like to see continued into the new millenium.

Assignment
- *The identified image will be described by each student in a short story which begins in the past and concludes sometime in the distant future.*
- *A collection of works which illustrate this image of women will be electronically scanned and used to illustrate the short story.*
- *A book jacket will be created using appropriate media.*

PRACTICE

GENDER ISSUES IN THE STUDIO

Feminist scholarship has caused many art teachers to stop and consider how gender informs student behaviours in their art studios.

Consider how the following gender issues are played out in your own classroom:

- **Visual Images**
  Do both male and female students feel free to depict non-stereotypical body images and subject matter in their art? Are you comfortable with their choices?

- **Role Models**
  Are female artists and art produced by women presented as part of the overall art curriculum or just within occasional units devoted to Women Artists?

- **Studio Tasks**
  Are male students expected to lift heavy objects and materials?
  Are female students responsible for cleaning up desks and sinks?

- **Studio Assignments**
  Do studio assignments reward:
  (a) competition over co-operation
  (b) originality over replication
  (c) tidiness over expressiveness?

TOPIC 16
FEMINISM

Whenever feminists put the spotlight on art education the picture framed is seldom very flattering. Young girls, in particular, reveal considerable levels of deep, internal conflict resulting from art curricula which demand assertive and competitive studio practices, and generally abrasive behaviours which contrast deeply with the socially-constructed feminine values of caring and nurturing.

FIRST GENERATION SCHOLARSHIP

Early feminists within the field of education focused their research along 3 distinct but allied lines: **social analysis**, **political activism**, and **self-knowledge**. In the first instance, studies were undertaken to determine how gender-differentiated patterns of schooling and maternally-based restrictions on career development negatively affected women. At the same time, political alliances at local, provincial, and national levels were forged with religious and labour organizations. Thirdly, female *ways of knowing* were used to advance pedagogies based upon co-operation and nurturance, and to promote qualitative research methodologies.

In the sub-field of art education, one of the easiest targets for feminists was the **dearth of women artists** and female-dominated art forms in standard art history texts. Sensitivity in this area has been raised significantly, however, research has shown that women artists 'of the past, the *lost women* so to speak, often gained prominence due to their aristocratic status or social relationship to practising male artists.

Increased **professional recognition** for women in art education was another key goal for early feminist scholarship. By the 1990s, gender parity had been achieved in professional art education organizations, publications, and graduate studies, where women actually outnumbered men at the doctoral level.

Feminists also noted the prevalence of **patriarchal female imagery** in art. The *male gaze*, they argued, involved much more than the traditional reclining female nude; it represented a systemic assumption within Western culture that the male experience was both universal and normative. In a related vein, feminists sought to redefine pornography to include any visual form of female subordination to men.

A fourth area of research explored **feminine aesthetic sensibility**. Proponents of a *gynecentric aesthetic* suggested that art created by women would characteristically promote greater viewer participation, traditional women's crafts, non-objectified female imagery, and co-operative studio production.

SECOND GENERATION SCHOLARSHIP

Second generation scholarship clearly shows the significant changes wrought by **postmodernist theory** in the overall feminist movement (*see Topic 15: Postmodernism*). Whereas early feminists often spoke in terms of gender superiority, second generation feminists speak primarily in terms of gender equality.

The Nature of Gender Difference
Contemporary data have demonstrated that modernist gender stereotypes and role definitions served men as badly as women, although in different ways. Certainly, rates of male incarceration, addiction, suicide, violence, and premature death belie the notion that life has always been so great for men. Modernist binaries like aggressor/victim, powerful/helpless, violent/passive, and abusive/nurturing, in which the former trait was invariably assigned to males and the latter to females, have been uncoupled and reconceptualized as human qualities which can affect both men and women.

Thus, the modernist male/female dichotomy has come under increasing scrutiny and feminists are now asking whether women are capable of assuming the role of privileged spectator and objectifying men:
- Can women produce pornographic art?
- Is there such as thing as a *female gaze*?

Reforming Art as a Discipline
Second generation feminists have also deconstructed traditional academic disciplines to reveal how they have historically favoured white males and, through exclusionary content and practices, disenfranchised virtually everybody else. Considerable attention has been paid to the ways in which works of art act as sites of ideological conflict in a corporate culture held together by networks of power and domination.

Drawing upon historical and ethnographic research methodologies, feminist art educators have sketched the outlines of a reformed art discipline which accommodates female ways of knowing and interacting. Key components of art curricula derived from such research include:
- a greater emphasis upon non-Western forms of artistic expression
- an increased sensitivity to the placement of artists in relevant cultural contexts
- a non-linear, non-progressive approach to art history
- a balance between formalist and alternative models of art criticism
- a shift in favour of co-operative, collaborative, and nurturing pedagogies.

FEMINISM & ART

- Collins, G., & Sandell, R. (Eds.). (1984). *Women, art and education.* Reston, VA: National Art Education Association.

- Collins, G., & Sandell, R. (Eds.). (1996). *Gender issues in art education: Content, contexts, and strategies.* Reston, VA: National Art Education Association.

- Glaser, J., & Zenetou, A. (Eds.). (1994). *Gender perspectives: Essays on women in museums.* Washington, DC: Smithsonian Institution Press.

- Irwin, R. (1995). *A circle of empowerment: Women, education, and leadership.* Albany, NY: State University of New York Press.

- Lather, P. (1991). *Getting smart: Feminist research and pedagogy within the post modern.* New York, NY: Routledge, Chapman and Hall.

- Saccá, E., & Zimmerman, E. (Eds.) (1998). *Herstories, ourstories, future stories.* Boucherville, PQ: Canadian Society for Education through Art.

Feminism / Topic 16 ■ 61 ■

PRACTICE

GLOBAL EDUCATION & ART

Advocates suggest that multiculturalism should not be considered a school subject *per se* but a pedagogic orientation which promotes cultural diversity throughout education. At the same time, however, they suggest that global education should be offered as a course in senior grades.

In their text *Global Teacher, Global Learner* Pike & Selby present these 4 dimensions to global education:

- **Spatial Dimension**
  Works of art should be analyzed for social, political, and economic qualities as well as stylistic influences.

- **Temporal Dimension**
  Works of art should speak to contemporary issues in addition to offering insights into the past.

- **Issues Dimension**
  Works of art should provide venues for discussing controversial issues such as AIDS, violence, and prejudice.

- **Human Dimension**
  Art curricula should stress that spiritual and emotional commitments are needed if we are to improve life on this planet.

TOPIC 17
MULTICULTURALISM

Multiculturalism has been official government policy in Canada for almost 30 years, however, the term itself is frequently misunderstood. The reason for this is very simple: multiculturalism can refer to a **political concept**, an **educational reform movement**, or a **socio-cultural process**. Even when multiculturalism is employed primarily in the context of an educational reform movement, confusion can still arise over the variety of differing philosophical approaches and curricular models. The dissenting voices of cultural assimilationists and separatists will also be addressed in this section.

APPROACHES TO MULTICULTURALISM

At the core of most multicultural curricula is a shared belief that Western culture oppresses minorities. Proponents of greater **cultural pluralism**, or ethnic diversity, generally adhere to one or other of the following 4 approaches to multiculturalism:

Attack Multiculturalism
Attack multiculturalists seek to expose the more oppressive features of Western society by drawing comparisons with more benign cultures. This approach is inherently the most negative of the four and, consequently, is the most likely to provoke strong reactions from mainstream groups and individuals.

Escape Multiculturalism
Escape multiculturalists are fond of exploring the exotic and heavily-romanticized cultures of relatively obscure and distant countries. This approach operates on the truism that familiarity breeds contempt, but often neglects to offer any practical way of incorporating these exotic features into Western society.

Transformative Multiculturalism
Transformative multiculturalists try to meld together the best features of diverse cultures to produce a hybrid society free of violence, oppression, or inequality. This approach is perhaps overly idealistic and does not adequately explain how the negative features of these diverse cultures can be avoided.

Repair Multiculturalism
Repair multiculturalists attempt to eliminate the social imbalances within Western culture by building the self-esteem of marginalized groups. While this approach succeeds in highlighting the achievements of minority groups, it too often assumes that Western minorities identify with their ancestral heritages.

DISSENTING VOICES

In the field of education, most provincial curriculum policies since the 1970s have echoed the federal government's support for official multiculturalism. As a result, the profession at-large has not been as actively engaged in debating the merits of alternative cultural perspectives as other segments of Canadian society. So, it may come as a bit of a shock to some teachers that not everybody thinks that multiculturalism is such a good idea. While at first glance alternative cultural perspectives may appear to vary widely among various marginalized groups, most of them can be grouped under the heading of either cultural assimilation or cultural separation.

Cultural Assimilation

Although cultural assimilation is often classified as a model of multiculturalism under the rubric of *teaching the exceptional and culturally different*, I believe that assimilationist curricula actually undermine the goals of multicultural education. Consequently, I have not included cultural assimilation among the models of multiculturalism presented on pages 64 & 65 (*see Stuhr, 1994 for more about this model*).

Assimilationist curricula assume that minorities will embrace Western culture once they have been introduced to its knowledge, skills, and aesthetic values. Critics assert that this approach implicitly links cultural conflict to **learning deficits in minority students** rather than inequities in Western society.

Cultural Separation

Opposition to multiculturalism also comes from a wide variety of groups who favour cultural separation. Cultural separatists share a common belief that official multiculturalism is little more than a cynical, political ruse designed by the ruling elite to maintain their dominance over restive but internally-divided minorities.

In Canada, support for cultural separation is most evident in **francophone and aboriginal communities** where multiculturalism is seen as a refusal by anglophones to accept Québec and First Nations peoples as equal partners within confederation.

Support for cultural separation is not limited, however, to just linguistic or racial minorities. Religious groups have also made claims for special status, especially in the field of education. As well, radical gays and lesbians have opted for cultural separatist movements such as *Queer Nation* and *Act-Up!* ∎

MULTICULTURALISM & ART

- Banks, J., & Banks, C. (1993). *Multicultural education: Issues and perspectives.* Boston, MA: Allyn & Bacon.

- Chalmers, G. (1996). *Celebrating pluralism: Art, education, and cultural diversity.* Los Angeles, CA: Getty Education Institute for the Arts.

- Goldberg, M. (1997). *Arts and learning: An integrated approach to teaching and learning in multicultural and multilingual settings.* Toronto, ON: Copp Clark Longman.

- Kauppinen H., & Diket, R. (Eds.). (1995). *Trends in art education from diverse cultures.* Reston, VA: National Art Education Association.

- Pike, G., & Selby, D. (1988). *Global teacher, global learner.* Toronto, ON: Hodder and Stoughton.

- Stuhr, P. (1994). Multicultural art education and social reconstruction. *Studies in Art Education, 35*(3), 171-178.

MODELS OF MULTICULTURALISM

HUMAN RELATIONS

CONCEPTUAL PREMISE

The human relations model adopts a repair approach to multiculturalism by highlighting the neglected achievements of various groups traditionally marginalized within mainstream Western culture. The model focuses on similarities among such groups and downplays areas of potential conflict.

CURRICULAR APPLICATION

Human relations curricula typically strive to improve levels of self-esteem, reduce the prevalence of negative cultural stereotypes, promote strong interpersonal relationships, and eliminate systemic sources of bias and prejudice. Art teachers are often asked to play an important role in such curricula by providing instructional activities which celebrate the holidays, festivals, and traditions of various minority groups.

PEDAGOGIC CONCERNS

Teachers need to ensure that curricula based on human relations:
- maintain the disciplinary integrity of art education through activities which provide authentic opportunities for growth in art production, art history, art criticism, and aesthetics
- present all works of art made by minority artists in ethnographically correct contexts
- avoid giving the impression that art education exists in schools only to decorate corridors and support more important subjects.

SINGLE GROUP STUDIES

CONCEPTUAL PREMISE

Conceptually similar to the human relations model, single group studies also celebrate the accomplishments of marginalized groups which often receive little recognition within mainstream culture. As the name implies, however, single group studies highlight only one minority at a time.

CURRICULAR APPLICATION

Curricula that promote the single group studies model of multiculturalism frequently draw heavily upon the knowledge and expertise of art teachers. Representative profiles of the minority group in question are gleaned through the careful analysis of artistic exemplars and artist biographies. Art works are also examined for any visual clues which might shed light on why the group has felt marginalized within Western culture.

PEDAGOGIC CONCERNS

Teachers need to ensure that curricula based on single group studies:
- avoid promoting escapist or nostaglic *Dances With Wolves/Lost Horizon* attitudes which suggest to students that they cannot make a difference in the real world
- focus on minority cultures which present issues and provide alternatives that have relevancy for Canadian students
- provide an honest, even-handed portrayal of both the accomplishments and weaknesses of the group under examination.

MULTICULTURAL EDUCATION

CONCEPTUAL PREMISE

Multicultural education is a comprehensive model that promotes cultural pluralism and social justice by reforming the overall school environment. Practically speaking, this involves hiring culturally-diverse employees and encouraging a co-operative, non-sexist approach to instructional activities.

CURRICULAR APPLICATION

Curricula designed to promote multicultural education are often planned around complex themes such as the exercise of power or the construction of knowledge, rather than traditional school subjects such as mathematics or science. Students are encouraged to bring their lived experiences into the classroom and evaluate the validity of the curriculum for themselves. Specialized expertise from members of the community is actively sought.

PEDAGOGIC CONCERNS

Teachers need to ensure that curricula based on multicultural education:
- resist pressures for stereotypical personnel assignments such as female family studies teachers, and avoid quota systems for hiring teachers or enrolling students
- provide clear strategies for dealing with the potentially explosive situations that arise when personal belief systems are challenged
- devise criteria for helping teachers and students decide what to include in the curriculum.

SOCIAL RECONSTRUCTION

CONCEPTUAL PREMISE

The social reconstruction model shares the same commitment to greater levels of cultural pluralism and social justice as multicultural education. The models differ, however, in their respective scope. Advocates of social reconstruction aim to reform society itself, not just the education system.

CURRICULAR APPLICATION

Social reconstruction curricula operate on a metacurricular level. Students from culturally marginalized groups are encouraged to investigate how social institutions work to their disadvantage; students from culturally dominant groups are encouraged to acknowledge the social dynamics which work to their advantage. Collectively, the students engage in various activities which have global and futures-oriented curricular objectives.

PEDAGOGIC CONCERNS

Teachers need to ensure that curricula based on social reconstruction:
- remain sensitive to and tolerant of students who come from excessively conservative or restrictive home environments, so that the students are not caught between the expectations of parents and teachers
- encourage students to strive for academic achievement with the same vigour as they work towards social improvement
- provide students with prospects for social change that are not unduly idealistic or dangerous. ■

PRACTICE

ACCESSING RESOURCES

Since the teaching profession generally does not have many First Nations people within its ranks, it is very important that teachers know how to access expertise from within First Nations communities. CSEA policies suggest these approaches:

- **Initiating Elder Participation**
  The first step involves sending a letter to the local Band Council requesting the assistance of an Elder in an educational activity. Your District Chiefs' Office, Tribal Council Office, Band Council, or Friendship Centre Education Committee can help you make this initial contact.

- **The Offering Cycle**
  In First Nations communities, it is customary to show respect and appreciation for knowledge by offering a gift to the participating Elder. The nature of such an offering varies among communities, so seek out local advice.

- **Respecting Sacred Artifacts**
  Should your educational activity involve the use or replication of any artifacts considered sacred by First Nations communities, accord the same reverence and respect that you would to artifacts used in your religious worship.

TOPIC 18
FIRST NATIONS ART

Our heightened awareness of the diversity of perspectives which exist within and among cultural groups is perhaps postmodernism's greatest contribution to contemporary Western society. For example, we pay scant attention today to research studies that speak of *men* in a global sense without taking into consideration other critical aspects such as race, age, class, or sexual orientation. Thus, we cannot even begin to address the art of First Nations communities without first acknowledging the cultural diversity that exists within and among Canada's native peoples.

CULTURAL DIVERSITY

Certainly the most important distinction to be made among First Nations communities concerns those situated on reserves and those located off-reserve in rural and urban municipalities. Generally speaking, natives on reserves have experienced greater success in resisting cultural assimilation and maintaining traditional cultural values. Not surprisingly, those who work or study off-reserve have suffered the greatest from conflicting cultural pressures.

Native cultures can be broadly classified into three groups: **traditional**, **transitional**, and **transformative** although public attention is generally focused upon traditional native groups living on remote reserves. Canadian art education researchers such as Rita Irwin and Elizabeth Saccá have studied traditional native communities and highlighted cultural distinctions that have special importance for art education.

Traditional Culture & Art
Traditional native languages do not have any equivalent for the Western concept of *art*, although it is certainly true that transitional and transformative communities have adapted Western aesthetics and media to produce a commercially viable art industry. Traditional native masks, for example, were made solely for spiritual ceremonies, never for decorative or aesthetic purposes.

Traditional Culture & Creativity
Traditional native languages do not have any equivalent for the Western concept of *creativity*, either; their closest approximations translate into English as *skilful* or *useful*. This traditional conception of the artist as a craftsperson, faithfully reproducing artifacts to transmit culture from one generation to the next, should not seem very unusual to us for it parallels the premodernist Western conception of the artist (*see Topic 11: The Artist*).

Traditional	made using ancestral techniques and media: ■ natural fibres, skins, bones, shells, glass beads used in traditional First Nations ceremonies conveys tribal resemblances rather than likenesses
Transitional	made using modern techniques and media: ■ yarn, cloth, plastic beads used in powwows and contemporary ceremonies designs are bolder and brighter than traditional
Transformative	made using modern techniques and media: ■ Western prints, sculptures, paintings often made for commercial enterprises reflects Western fine art aesthetics and values

18.1
FIRST NATIONS ART
Classes

FIRST NATIONS ART

■ Assembly of First Nations. (1988). *Tradition and education: Towards a vision of our future. A declaration of First Nations' jurisdiction over education.* Ottawa, ON: Author.

■ Bennett, B., & Hall, C. (1984). *Discovering Canadian art: Learning the language.* Toronto, ON: Prentice Hall.

■ Long, D., & Dickason, O. (Eds.). (1996). *Visions of the heart: Canadian aboriginal issues.* Toronto, ON: Harcourt Brace.

■ MacGregor, R., Hall, C., Bennett, B., & Calvert, A. (1987). *Canadian art: Building a heritage.* Toronto, ON: Prentice Hall.

■ Rogers, L. (1993). *Chapter images: General facts on Navajo chapters.* Window Rock, Navajo Nation: Division of Community Development.

■ Stuhr, P. (1987). Cultural conflict: Viewed through the art of the contemporary Wisconsin Indians. *Dissertation Abstracts International, 48,* 9-2226.

PEDAGOGIC CONSIDERATIONS

While it is indeed important to highlight such distinctions, it is also necessary to balance lessons about traditional culture with activities that expose students to transitional and transformative art and artists. Care must be taken to research, select, and present native exemplars in culturally-appropriate contexts, especially when religious artifacts are involved.

Teachers should not assume that students of First Nations heritage self-identify with traditional cultural values and practices, since they might be just as immersed in Western culture as non-native students. In the literature, this process is known as **pedagogic erasure**.

Finally, while avoiding overly-romanticized versions of First Nations cultures, teachers need to draw attention to such unique aspects as native conceptions of history as circular and repetitive, preference for continuity over innovation, and emphasis on groups rather than individuals. ■

TOPIC 19
GAY & LESBIAN ART

ADDRESSING HOMOPHOBIA

American art educator Laurel Lampela has offered the following pedagogic strategies for addressing homophobia:

- **Recognizing Abuse**
  Take immediate action when slurs are overheard. Make it clear that hurtful words will not be allowed in your classroom.

- **Speaking Up**
  Accept that addressing homophobia requires action from heterosexual individuals and groups. For example, speak up whenever friends or colleagues make disparaging comments about gays or lesbians.

- **Gaining Awareness**
  Make an effort to learn more about gay and lesbian lifestyles. You will discover that they can be as diverse as those found in straight society.

- **Developing Sensitivity**
  Be sensitive to educational activities and environments which are inappropriate for gay or lesbian students. Wherever possible, provide alternatives which more fully maintain personal dignity and safety.

A lthough *the love that dares not speak its name* has found a voice in most forms of artistic expression, homosexuality has barely managed a whisper in art education. Fearful of incurring the wrath of parents or school administrators, most teachers have continued to employ subtle forms of self-censorship. Similarly, biographical sketches in most art history texts used in schools still reflect an academic version of the U.S. military's *don't ask - don't tell* policy. For example, in a section describing Michelangelo's well-known and unmistakably homoerotic statue *David*, Janson's *A Basic History of Art* notes that Michelangelo "had just spent several years in Rome and had been strongly impressed with the emotion-filled, muscular bodies of Hellenistic sculpture" (1986, p. 212). *Well, when in Rome ..*

POSTMODERNIST INFLUENCES

Up until the late 1980s, the sparse references to gays and lesbians in art education journals had been limited to such dark topics as AIDS, pornography, or moral degeneracy. Since the formation of gay and lesbian caucuses in the American Federation of Teachers, the National Education Association, The College Art Association, the Alliance for Museum Education and the National Art Education Association, however, entirely new voices have begun speaking up in such respected professional publications as the *Journal of the Canadian Society for Education through Art*, *Studies in Art Education*, and *Art Education.*

Gender & Sexuality
The immense contributions made by early feminist scholars to postmodernist theory tended to obscure more subtle forms of cultural oppression. By focusing their discourse upon male/female social conflict, distinctions between gender identity and sexual orientation often remained inadequately addressed. More radical gay and lesbian activists sought to fill this void through **cultural separatist movements** such as *Queer Nation* and **political advocacy groups** such as *Act-Up!*

Under Reconstruction
The postmodernist concept of reconstruction suggests that since cultural phenomena are interpreted through personal perspectives, or **world views**, they are of necessity diverse and often contradictory. Increased exposure through consumer-oriented media outlets has led to a greater awareness within the general population that gay and lesbian lifestyles can often match the diversity found in straight society. With the advent of a new millenium upon them, many gays and lesbians remain divided between those who reject mainstream culture outright and those who desire even greater levels of public acceptance.

PEDAGOGIC CONSIDERATIONS

Do our students need to know whether or not Michelangelo was gay in order to fully appreciate *David*?

Theoretical Responses

Art scholars involved in historical research generally fall into one or other of two opposing camps. **Essentialists** maintain that since homosexual artists have existed in virtually every culture we can indeed speak of gay aesthetic sensibilities or visual subtexts. **Social reconstructionists**, however, suggest that impugning such sensibilities or subtexts to historical works of art is patently anachronistic. While it is clearly true that homosexuals have produced great works of art in the past, there have been few, if any, historical parallels to contemporary Western gay culture. So, any mention of a particular artist's sexual orientation is, at best, extraneous information or, at worst, misleading propaganda.

Proponents of **modernist art** would probably answer this question by suggesting that issues of sexual orientation seldom need addressing, since the formal properties of art objects are far more important than any subject matter intended by the artist or perceived by the viewer. On the other hand, advocates of **postmodernist art** would likely say that Michelangelo's sexual orientation represents a critical factor in our understanding of *David*'s original meaning and its deconstruction by gay or straight viewers.

Personal Responses

For many teachers, however, such theoretical arguments cannot help them answer the question at-hand; instead, the relevance of Michelangelo's sexual orientation can only be resolved on a personal basis. For those teaching within excessively conservative communities or parochial school systems, introducing such a controversial topic could be seen as an assault on family values or a rejection of religious beliefs. Alongside such professional constraints, however, are some equally pervasive professional obligations. One does not have to teach art to be aware that homosexual students exist in every classroom, or that heterosexual students often have gay or lesbian family members. I believe that as educators we have an obligation to provide inclusive and supportive learning environments for these students, as well.

Controversial Imagery in the Classroom

In the next section of this text, I will speak more directly to the pedagogic issues related to controversial art. Special attention will be paid to the historic use of nude models by artists throughout Western art. A few, simple strategies for introducing such imagery into the classroom will be presented. ∎

GAYS, LESBIANS, & ART

- Boffin, T., & Fraser, J. (Eds.). (1991). *Stolen glances: Lesbians take photographs.* London, UK: Pandora.

- Cooper, E. (1994). *The sexual perspective: Homosexuality and art in the last 100 years in the west.* London, UK: Routledge & Kegan Paul.

- Kaiser, C. (1997). *The gay metropolis.* New York, NY: Houghton Mifflin.

- Kelley, C. (Ed.). (1992). *Forbidden subjects: Self-portraits by lesbian artists.* North Vancouver, BC: Gallerie.

- Pratt, A. (1997). (Ed.). *The critical response to Andy Warhol.* Westport, CT: Greenwood.

- Russo, V. (1987). *The celluloid closet* (rev. ed.). New York, NY: Harper & Row.

- Weinberg, J. (1993). *Speaking for vice: Homosexuality in the art of Charles Demuth, Marsden Hartley, and the first American avant-garde.* New Haven, CT: Yale University Press.

PRACTICE

UNDERSTANDING CENSORSHIP

Censorship presents an educational issue that can be most effectively covered within interdisciplinary studies. The following lesson ideas involve art, political science, religious education, and technology:

- **The Iconoclasts**
  What did the iconoclasts do during:
  (a) the Byzantine empire
  (b) the Protestant reformation?
  Can you think of any contemporary examples of iconoclastic activity?

- **The Art Police**
  Research the following attempts to censor controversial images:
  (a) Motion Picture Production Code
  (b) cable television V-chip
  (c) Internet blocking devices.
  Discuss the *pros* and *cons* in each case.

- **The Censorship Game**
  Divide your students into groups and have them prepare a cultural manifesto outlining 5 fundamental social values for an imaginary nation. Ask each group to identify 5 Canadian works of art which could be displayed in their national art gallery and 5 which would be banned. Each group should be prepared to defend their decisions using the values described in their manifesto.

TOPIC 20
CONTROVERSIAL ART

Ideas are power. Whether written, spoken, or drawn, ideas can defeat even the darkest oppression. Since all three of these sources of power come together in the art room, we should not be surprised to encounter situations where individuals or groups try to control the art curricula in our schools. Although controversial ideas found in novels and textbooks are more easily labeled as obscene than images found in portfolios, art teachers must use professional judgement in the selection of exemplars, use of models, and discussion of hiddenstream art. Too often, however, the exercise of professional judgement has translated into widespread self-censorship and the avoidance of anything controversial. I believe such strategies do our students a great disservice by removing educational opportunities for practising critical **thinking** skills, developing **respect** for others, and acquiring a **tolerance** for diversity.

PROFESSIONAL STRATEGIES

Guiding Children
Discussions about artistic censorship in public spaces such as galleries or city parks do not provide much guidance to teachers, especially those in elementary schools where young children are involved. Gallery docents may be able to show controversial photographs by Robert Mapplethorpe in a room which fully-advised, adult patrons have chosen to enter but classrooms are very different. Teachers are much like **parents**, they make decisions based on the best interests of children (*see Topic 1: The Art Studio*). Our culturally diverse schools, however, require teachers to be many different parents at the same time. Teachers must, therefore, anticipate occasional conflicts with parents and community groups.

Building Support
In many cases, concerns about the introduction of controversial ideas in art curricula can be avoided by simply keeping the lines of **communication** open with principals, parents, and community groups. Although school administrators do not generally come from art backgrounds, they can be surprisingly supportive if sensitized to the principles of art education through classroom visits and student displays. Similarly, an explanatory letter sent home to parents before the introduction of controversial material can make all the difference and provide an opportunity for parents to help prepare the children.

Handling Complaints
Sometimes conflicts are unavoidable. Ideally, complaints should be handled by a previously established review committee. Recommendations should be clearly transmitted to the classroom teacher, who will work co-operatively with the complainant(s) to devise an alternative activity for the student(s) involved.

NUDE or NAKED

Controversial imagery in art can focus on a wide range of issues such as religion, politics, or violence but the human body is the most enduring because it provides a point of convergence for all of these. Distinctions made between serious portrayals of a **nude model** and erotic exploitations of a **naked body** have consistently lost out to Christian teachings which associate the human body with sin and shame. In recent decades, however, religious concerns have been overtaken by those of politics and violence. Feminists have linked the widespread abuse of women to the objectification of women in Western art. The **male gaze** has been coined to describe this dynamic in which female imagery is controlled by men. Increased media exposure to gays and lesbians has also affected public sensibilities to nude imagery.

PEDAGOGIC CONSIDERATIONS

Figure 20.1 *Seated Nude Wearing Boots*, to the right, also appears on page 25 as an illustrative example of a Grade 11 assignment in extended figure drawing.

- Would you have shown this exemplar to a Grade 11 art class in your school? If not, why not?

- Would you use a nude model in such an assignment? Would it make any difference if the model were male or female?

- Would you display a similar drawing that had been completed by a student:
  (a) in the art room
  (b) in the hallway of your school
  (c) in the board of education building
  (d) in the local shopping mall?

- How would you respond to a parental complaint over such an assignment or display?

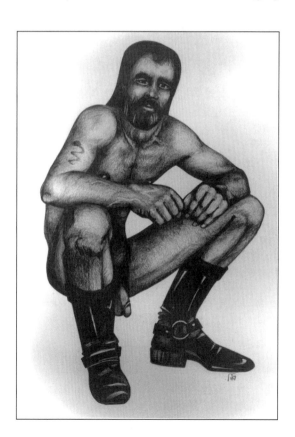

CONTROVERSY & ART

- Bolton, R. (Ed.). (1992). *Culture wars*. New York, NY: The New Press.

- Booth, D. (1992). *Censorship goes to school.* Markham, ON: Pembroke.

- Dubin, S. (1992). *Arresting images.* New York, NY: Routledge, Chapman and Hall.

- Marsh, D. (1991). *50 ways to fight censorship.* New York, NY: Thunder's Mouth Press.

20.1
ROGER CLARK
Seated Nude Wearing Boots 1987
Graphite on paper
45.5 x 61 cm.
Collection of the artist

PRACTICE

LESSON IDEAS

- **Gone With the Wind**
  Write a play about the adventures of a family traveling in a hot air balloon. Where did they come from? Why did they want to leave? Where did they hope to land? Who lived there already?

- **Transformers**
  Reconstruct this object in 3-D using appropriate mixed media.

- **Some Assembly Required**
  Research other versions of early aircraft design, especially those envisaged by Classical and Renaissance inventors.

- **The A Files**
  Does life exist on other planets? Depict a landscape from one such world.

- **Ticket to Ride**
  Try to envisage a mode of transportation that does not yet exist, such as a vehicle for traveling to the centre of the Earth or through time to the year 3000 A.D. Draw this vehicle from two perspectives along with explanatory, didactic notes.

- **Airships Then & Now**
  What famous airship crashed in 1937? Are lighter-than-air craft used today?

GUIDE 1
GALLERY 1

Plate 1
JOHN MacGREGOR
Interplanetary Voyage 1967
Graphite, acrylic, and tempera on paper
91.4 x 111.8 cm.
Collection of the McIntosh Gallery
The University of Western Ontario
Purchase, Centennial Grant from the
Province of Ontario, 1967

SUBJECT MATTER

Working sketches are usually tossed away into a recycling basket once **extended work** is finished, however, they are frequently considered works of art in their own right as we see in *Interplanetary Voyage*. The subject matter for this **surrealist** work can be easily ascertained from the **didactic notes** written by John MacGregor in the lower-right corner:

"Interplanetary Voyage - Lana's oft-printed airship (1744)/ Lana a Jesuit Priest pointed out the potential/ military use of flying machines as bombers or/ troop carriers - these views have been said/ to explain why Lana never attempted to construct/ a model of his airship design./ Best of Luck/ Father Lana/ Yours truly XXX/ Deanna Paira & John MacGregor."

ELEMENTS OF COMPOSITION

Colour
The whimsical character of *Interplanetary Voyage* is reinforced by the use of brilliant, pure colours in the **primary hues** of red, blue, and yellow. This basic colour palette is reminiscent of **symbolic child art** (*see Topic 2: Art Development*). After all, who else but a child would imagine traveling to another planet by rowing through the air in a boat held aloft by balloons .. *a Jesuit priest living in 1744?*

Line
MacGregor has relied almost completely on the element of colour for constructing this imaginary craft, however, it is interesting to note his use of **outlines** to define most of the key shapes. As a general rule, such drawn elements are rarely used in paintings, where changes in colour are used to delineate shape. Again, one is reminded of children's drawing books when keeping inside the lines is *de rigeur*, although the frequent use of outlines in paintings by postimpressionist Paul Gauguin also comes to mind.

PRINCIPLES OF COMPOSITION

Balance
Plate 1 presents a clear illustration of a combined **symmetrical/asymmetrical balance**. The absence of any objects on the right side of the picture surface makes it easy to focus on the visual weight of the only significant element to be balanced in *Interplanetary Voyage* - the craft itself. By visually estimating axis lines which horizontally and vertically balance the main image, we can see that the craft is balanced symmetrically about the horizontal axis and asymmetrically about the vertical. The vertical balance divides the work into 1/3 to the left and 2/3 to the right - a ratio which approximates **the golden mean**.

Emphasis
In order to emphasize the idea of traveling through air, as well as to reinforce the surrealism of the craft, MacGregor has left the background largely empty; as a result, the work is not situated within the real world in any traditional sense. One exception to this involves the blue paint which surrounds the boat, although it is not clear if the blue is intended to represent a body of water or the expansive sky. ∎

RESEARCH

JOHN MacGREGOR
b. 1944 Dorking, Sussex, England

John MacGregor was an active member of the artistic community in Toronto where he taught at the Ontario College of Art. Currently, John MacGregor resides in the United States.

STYLISTIC INFLUENCES

Interplanetary Voyage provides us with a clear example of **surrealistic expression** of reality. Stylistically it can be classified as **fantasy** (*see page 46*).

The work is reminiscent of Leonardo da Vinci's sketches for lighter-than-air craft. Lana's proposed airship is characteristic of many works of fantasy in that it tries to portray an imaginary object using realistic components.

Lana's concern about military uses for his flying machine suggests an underlying fear of the unknown and a deep distrust of human nature, two expressive qualities which are commonly found in surrealistic art.

PRACTICE

LESSON IDEAS

- **Background Check**
  Replace the checkerboard background in Plate 2 with one of your own choice. How does the new background affect your interpretation of this work?

- **B-Girls**
  Write a short story based on the interaction between Betty and Beryl.

- **The Substitute**
  Reproduce Plate 2 in the media of your choice, however, replace one of the persons with a character that is either male or elderly. How does this alter the meaning of the original work?

- **Art, She Wrote**
  Become a famous art sleuth and analyze Plate 2 for visual cues related to gender, race, and class.

- **Scenes From a Mall**
  Conduct response interviews to this work from individuals shopping in a local mall. Analyze the data by gender, race, age, and, if possible, by religion or sexual orientation. What conclusions can you draw from your data collection? Has the research changed your own opinions about Plate 2?

GUIDE 2
GALLERY 2

Plate 2
DENNIS BURTON
Newark, New Jersey, July 11 1967 or
Across the Peace Bridge 1968
Oil on canvas
152.7 x 152.7 cm.
Collection of the McIntosh Gallery
The University of Western Ontario
Purchase, Board of Governors, 1968

SUBJECT MATTER

What is going on in Plate 2? Although contemporary viewers might come up with a variety of answers to this query, clues to Dennis Burton's original intent reside within the lengthy title of this **realistic** work: *Newark, New Jersey, July 11 1967 or Across the Peace Bridge*. For members of Generation X, some quick research will reveal that Newark, New Jersey experienced violent, racial clashes in the summer of 1967. The intended subject matter, therefore, was **racial oppression**. According to the artist, the narrative involved two women named Beryl and Betty. Beryl, on the left, was an educated, white socialite while Betty, on the right, was an impoverished, black domestic. In Plate 2 Betty has been ordered to put on Beryl's shoes. Humiliated, she is tempted to push Beryl onto the floor. What do you think happened?

ELEMENTS OF COMPOSITION

Colour
Plate 2 is unusual in that Burton has introduced a few splashes of colour into what is basically a study in black & white. The squares of pure colour in the background, along the bottom and right edge, signify the inherent equality of different racial groups. The only other significant use of colour in this painting has been reserved for the undergarments worn by Beryl, the dominant woman with wealth and power. Thus, three key areas of postmodernist theory · **gender**, **race**, and **class** · have been tagged for attention within this predominantly modernist painting.

Shape
A sense of visual depth has been achieved in this painting by Beryl's extended right leg. When shapes appear to be at right angles to the picture plane, they are said to be **foreshortened**. Close inspection of this part of the painting reveals that the shoe has more definition and heavily contrasted values than any other area. This is called **aerial perspective** and it increases our sense of overall visual depth.

PRINCIPLES OF COMPOSITION

Balance
What part of this painting first caught your eye? Personally, I looked at Beryl's left leg which advances from the picture plane. This **major focal point** is also where the two central figures in this narrative almost come into contact with each other. If we locate this focal point halfway between the two hands on Beryl's leg, the picture is divided horizontally 2/3 above and 1/3 below, and vertically 2/3 to the left and 1/3 to the right. Plate 2, therefore, is an example of **asymmetrical** balance. The faces of the two women provide **minor focal points**; collectively, the three focal points produce a **triangular scan path**.

Contrast
Contrasting elements are found throughout this painting. In terms of **composition**, we have contrasts in shape, colour, and value; in **subject matter**, we have contrasts in gender, race, and class. ∎

RESEARCH

DENNIS BURTON
b. 1933 Lethbridge, Alberta, Canada

Dennis Burton has had a major impact on contemporary Canadian art, receiving four Canada Council awards and winning many national and international competitions. Currently, he is a studio instructor at the Emily Carr Institute in British Columbia.

STYLISTIC INFLUENCES

Newark, New Jersey, July 11 1967 or Across the Peace Bridge is an example of **realistic expression** of reality. Stylistically it can be classed as **new realism** (*see page 47*).

This work contains several visual elements which are characteristic of new realism. Technically similar to Philip Pearlstein's *Female Model on Platform Rocker*, the realistic modeling of the nearly nude women shows a departure from modernist representations of the human figure.

The pop art background provides both a stylistic link to modernism and a contrast to the postmodernist subject matter.

PRACTICE

LESSON IDEAS

- **Change That Style**
  How many characteristics of abstract art can you identify in Plate 3? Select a realistic painting of your own choice and reproduce it using all of the abstract elements employed by kerry ferris.

- **My Mother the Icon**
  The mother-and-child theme has been a favourite of artists from virtually all cultures. Research non-Western examples and compare them to Christian *Madonna and Child* icons.

- **No Animals Allowed**
  Artworks which depict animals in naturalistic settings, such as those by Canadian Robert Bateman, are often shunned by *avant-garde* critics and are rarely shown in contemporary art galleries. Why? Can illustrative works be considered art? What criteria can you offer to defend your position?

- **Once More With Feeling**
  Are you left with a sympathetic response to this depiction of nature? Research other works which present nature in positive, neutral, and negative lights. How have these works managed to evoke such diverse viewpoints?

GUIDE 3
GALLERY 3

Plate 3
kerry ferris
sunset - metamorphosis one 1985/86
Watercolour on paper
54.5 x 66.5 cm.
Collection of the artist

SUBJECT MATTER

Over the past few years, it has become common to see names printed solely in lowercase. In some instances, this decision to reject the conventional use of uppercase letters for proper names indicates a feminist perspective. kerry ferris, however, uses lowercase letters to reflect her ardent belief in the spiritual equality of all living beings, plant or animal. This **spiritual equality** is certainly evident in her **abstract** painting *sunset - metamorphosis one*. The subject matter is clearly centred upon maternal bonding; the orangutan and its baby are actually self-portraits of the artist and her son. ferris regularly involves exotic locales and endangered species in her work - elements often devalued and destroyed by Western culture. In Plate 3 ferris's choice of nontraditional subject matter is complemented by her unconventional use of colour, shape, and value. As well, her decision not to suggest any linear or aerial perspective gives this painting an intentionally vague sense of object placement and visual depth.

ELEMENTS OF COMPOSITION

Colour
Abstract art very often involves the use of **block colours** - areas of colour which remain consistent. Normally, colours in art are modulated by changes in either **intensity** (*brightness/dullness*), **value** (*lightness/darkness*), or **hue** (*blending with another colour*) to more closely resemble the subtle changes that areas of colour undergo in the natural world. In *sunset - metamorphosis one* kerry ferris has paired **complementary** block colours to achieve an abnormally high degree of colour contrast and vibrancy. Complementary colours, such as red and green, are located opposite each other on a colour wheel. When blended with green, red becomes duller; when placed adjacent to green, red appears brighter. We can see how effective the pairing of red and green can be in the upper background of this work.

Shape
Another characteristic of many abstract works is the use of **block shapes**. This greater consistency of shape can be achieved in a number of ways. For example, the immense diversity of realistic objects can be reduced by substituting regular, geometric forms for irregular, organic shapes, and by replacing gradual changes in surface with hard edges.

PRINCIPLES OF COMPOSITION

Balance
In Gallery 1, 2, & 4 the principle of balance is discussed primarily in relation to the element of shape. Compositional balance may be achieved, however, with any of the other elements as well. In this work we can detect balance through **line** (*the horizontal bands in the background counter the verticality of the animals in the foreground*) and **colour** (*the use of paired complementaries*).

Movement
I can almost feel the wind blowing in the background of kerry ferris' *sunset - metamorphosis one*, can you? This implied movement of leaves and branches has been achieved by her **repetition** of stratified blocks of intense, complementary colours, and sweeping, horizontal lines. ∎

kerry ferris
b. 1949 London, Ontario, Canada

From her art studio in London, Ontario kerry ferris has traveled to the Canadian Arctic, Ecuador, Portugal, Zimbabwe, and the Galapagos Islands in a quest to learn more about the landscape, people, and animals of distant lands.

STYLISTIC INFLUENCES

sunset - metamorphosis one offers a good example of **abstract expression** of reality. Stylistically it comes under the heading of **expressionism** (*see page 48*).

Although *sunset - metamorphosis one* relies on the postimpressionist blocks of colour we see in Paul Gauguin's *Mahana No Atua*, its overwhelming sense of rhythm places it closer to expressionistic compositions such as Emily Carr's *Study in Movement* and Franz Marc's *The Great Blue Horses*.

ferris has added a postmodernist element to this expressionistic work, however, with her emphasis upon the spiritual equality of plants and animals.

PRACTICE

LESSON IDEAS

- **The Shape of Music**
  Option 1: Produce a non-objective monoprint which illustrates your favourite piece of music. Be prepared to justify your use of visual elements.
  Option 2: Produce a 30- to 60-second musical sound track for Plate 4.

- **Doomsday 2000**
  As the end of the millenium approached, many Western societies witnessed a surge in the popularity of doomsday cults. Research such cults of the recent and not-so-recent past for similarities and differences. How have artists depicted apocalyptic visions of the future?

- **I ♥ Haiku**
  Compose a haiku poem for Bob Zarski's *Millenium.*

- **Brave New World**
  Do you have a favourite novel about the future? Classic stories such as *Animal Farm, Brave New World, Fahrenheit 451, The Time Machine, The Chrysalids,* and *Zardoz* are probably available in your local library. Construct a clay model of a person, animal, building, or vehicle from your novel.

GUIDE 4
GALLERY 4

Plate 4
BOB ZARSKI
Millenium 1980
Acrylic on canvas
76.2 x 101.6 cm.
Collection of the McIntosh Gallery
The University of Western Ontario
Purchase, McIntosh Fund, 1981

SUBJECT MATTER

As is the case with all **non-objective** works of art, *Millenium* is devoid of any truly realistic subject matter. In the absence of the usual, reassuring collection of people, animals, and plants, we have only the pure **elements of composition** with which to react and find personal meaning. Nonetheless, since *Millenium* provides us with a veritable explosion of enticing visual elements, most notably shape, colour, and value, it is almost impossible not to be drawn to this electrifying painting by Bob Zarski.

When confronted with non-objective art, I always prefer to form a personal, emotional response to the work in advance of reading the title assigned by the artist. I encourage teachers to adopt this approach with their own students by brainstorming a list of **adjectives** or **adverbs** upon their first exposure to a non-objective work. It is interesting to see how appropriate their lists frequently turn out to be when the actual title is revealed. What list could we produce for Plate 4? How about *busy, hectic, futuristic, cramped,* or *inter-galactic*? Not a bad match for what Zarski obviously intended us to sense in *Millenium.*

ELEMENTS OF COMPOSITION

Shape

Zarski has taken great care in delineating the myriad of shapes in *Millenium*. At first glance, this high level of detail tricks us into assuming that realistic objects can be readily identified. Upon closer examination, however, it becomes clear that none of the objects can actually be labeled with certainty. Just as we find ourselves on the verge of declaring a shape to be something realistic, it undergoes a metamorphosis into another shape. Thus, we find ourselves confronted with a new visual challenge and the process begins all over again. This human desire to link something familiar to the unknown, coupled with the underlying **serpentine design**, produces a **circular scan path** that passes over every part of this visually complex work - regardless of where we first begin to look.

Value

The black & white reproduction of *Millenium* found on page 78 clearly shows the important role played by value. A sense of **visual depth** within the picture plane and an impression of **three-dimensionality** within the curvilinear shapes have been achieved by using a complete range of value and by placing contrasting values next to each other.

PRINCIPLES OF COMPOSITION

Balance

Plate 4 provides us with an excellent example of **informal balance**. Compositional elements such as shape and colour have been distributed with relatively equal emphases throughout the picture surface. As a result, *Millenium* does not have an obvious **focal point**; instead, the entire work has been treated as a singular **focal area**. The visual weight of the densely compacted shapes is roughly centred in the middle of the work.

Movement

A sense of movement has been achieved within Plate 4 by the **repetition of similar shapes**, and by the **absence of a focal point** around which the visual elements might be fixed and lent a more static quality. You just can't remain looking at only one area of *Millenium* for any length of time. ■

RESEARCH

BOB (Bogdan) ZARSKI
b. 1949 Neustadt, Germany

A practising artist for 30 years, Bob Zarski describes himself as a colourist whose interpretive paintings owe their inspiration to literary works. Zarski has adopted an *accumulative* process to art production wherein his paintings emerge directly on the canvas - working sketches aren't used.

STYLISTIC INFLUENCES

Millenium demonstrates a **non-objective expression** of reality. Stylistically it can best be considered **pop art** (*see page 49*).

Although the compositional exuberance of *Millenium* might bear a visual resemblance to abstract expressionistic paintings by Jackson Pollock or Jean-Paul Riopelle, in terms of technique *Millenium* could hardly be more distanced from action painting. Zarski's carefully constructed web of crafted shapes and contrasted colours stands poles apart from the kinesthetic approach used in abstract expressionism. *Millenium* provides a clear reminder that styles of expression can encompass a truly broad range of different studio processes.

REPRODUCTIONS

Plate 1
JOHN MacGREGOR
Interplanetary Voyage 1967
Graphite, acrylic, and tempera on paper
91.4 x 111.8 cm.
Collection of the McIntosh Gallery
The University of Western Ontario
Purchase, Centennial Grant from the Province of Ontario, 1967

Plate 2
DENNIS BURTON
Newark, New Jersey, July 11 1967 or Across the Peace Bridge 1968
Oil on canvas
152.7 x 152.7 cm.
Collection of the McIntosh Gallery
The University of Western Ontario
Purchase, Board of Governors, 1968

Plate 3
kerry ferris
sunset - metamorphosis one 1985/86
Watercolour on paper
54.5 x 66.5 cm.
Collection of the artist

Plate 4
BOB ZARSKI
Millenium 1980
Acrylic on canvas
76.2 x 101.6 cm.
Collection of the McIntosh Gallery
The University of Western Ontario
Purchase, McIntosh Fund, 1981

2.2
TODD
I am Swimming in the Pool
Tempera on paper
45.5 x 61 cm.
Collection of J.H. Martin

2.4
TODD
I am Building a Snowman
Tempera on paper
45.5 x 61 cm.
Collection of J.H. Martin

2.6
TODD
We are Riding on a Double-Decker Bus
Tempera on paper
45.5 x 61 cm.
Collection of J.H. Martin

5.1
ROGER CLARK
Seated Nude Wearing Boots 1987
Graphite on paper
45.5 x 61 cm.
Collection of the artist

20.1
ROGER CLARK
Seated Nude Wearing Boots 1987
Graphite on paper
45.5 x 61 cm
Collection of the artist

2.3
TODD
It's a Design
Tempera on paper
45.5 x 61 cm.
Collection of J.H. Martin

2.5
TODD
I am Playing in the Garden
Tempera on paper
45.5 x 61 cm.
Collection of J.H. Martin

14.1
ROGER CLARK
Genesis Revisited 1982
Plaster and vermiculite
66 x 46 cm.
Collection of the artist

C.1
ROGER CLARK
Genesis Revisited 1982
Plaster and vermiculite
66 x 46 cm.
Collection of the artist

PHOTOGRAPHY

Plate 1, 2, 3, & 4   Grimes Photography, Inc., London, Ontario
5.1, 14.1, 20.1, & C.1 Media Services, Faculty of Education, The University of Western Ontario   ■